One Boy's Struggle:

A Memoir

Surviving Life With

Undiagnosed ADD

(Attention Deficit Disorder)

By

Bryan L. Hutchinson

ISBN 0-7414-4440-2

Published by:

INFIƆ🜊ITY
PUBLISHING.COM

1094 New DeHaven Street, Suite 100
West Conshohocken, PA 19428-2713
Info@buybooksontheweb.com
www.buybooksontheweb.com
Toll-free (877) BUY BOOK
Local Phone (610) 941-9999
Fax (610) 941-9959

Printed in the United States of America

Printed on Recycled Paper

Published June 2008

Dedicated to my wife,

Joan Faith Hutchinson

Contents

Foreword

This book is an endeavor to help others understand the disorders called Attention Deficit Disorder (ADD) and Attention Deficit Hyperactivity Disorder (ADHD). Because these two disorders are so similar to one another, they are often referenced together as ADD/HD. When you see this acronym, please know that whatever you're reading refers to either ADD/HD or both simultaneously. For that purpose, (and for simplicity's sake) throughout this book I'll be doing the same.

In telling this story of my life with undiagnosed ADD, I want to give insight to others about the suffering and difficulties a person could be faced with while having a disorder and not knowing it. You or someone close to you may have been diagnosed with ADD/HD, or perhaps you suspect that it is present but there has been no diagnosis. By telling my story, I will be sharing the difficulties that someone with undiagnosed ADD/HD goes through, being and feeling misunderstood and how significant those difficulties can be. I'll also reveal the great relief and liberation I found through a proper diagnosis and treatment. I want to help parents, guardians, friends, teachers, and spouses understand this disorder better from sharing my experiences. Through understanding, others can hopefully gain some insight and find help and solutions for those who may be affected by ADD/HD directly or indirectly.

By the time a doctor diagnosed me with ADD, I was already thirty-seven years old. The diagnosis proved to be liberating, however it was also infuriating knowing I had lived a life of intense struggle which could possibly have been avoided. With an earlier diagnosis, my experiences could have been vastly different. I might have been treated with understanding and consideration instead of blame and punishment. Living with undiagnosed ADD/HD not only affected me, but also those around me. I am not an authority on these learning disabilities; I am only telling the story of my life and sharing my opinions. I give suggestions on what I consider better ways of living with ADD/HD, which I have learned through therapy, research, trial and error, close friends, and the loving care and concern of my wife. I will also explain how letting my boss know that I have ADD improved my work relationships and my performance. Of course, anyone who suspects they may have any kind of illness or disability should see a doctor.

My wife has sincere and serious concerns about me writing this book and revealing the harsh realities of my past. She is worried about the possible negative repercussions from publishing this book. Her concerns are valid and there is a possibility that people will ridicule me for writing about my experiences and respond negatively toward me knowing that I have ADD. Still, I know there are kids and adults out there with ADD/HD who don't know it. They unnecessarily may be living emotionally difficult lives, and I take that to heart. I know what it's like to grow up misunderstood by my parents, teachers and friends, and even myself, for the way I am. I want to help others in some way to not have to go through what I went through as a child. If telling my story can do that, then I am not concerned with the potential negative repercussions I may receive from others. My wife does not have ADD, but she has lived through the negative treatment of people for things she has done, or simply for being who she is, and would prefer I not suffer the same or worse. I love her even more for her concern for my well-being, and we both agree it is even more important to help others. There is still a stigma to admitting to and having ADD/HD. Having any kind of disability or mental illness is still viewed as a disadvantage socially and professionally, therefore many people delay or do not seek medical advice or treatment for themselves or their children as a result. There are also people who do not agree that ADD/HD exists and believe that it is used as a cop-out or an excuse for distractive, inattentive, or lazy behavior. These misconceptions deter many individuals from seeking help, possibly preventing them from living more fulfilling lives. Even if you feel as though the majority of people might be against you, why add yourself to the list? A million people's disapproval might seem insurmountable to overcome, but it is not. What is insurmountable is when you add yourself to that list and make the disapproving ranks stronger. Self-doubt is often the hardest obstacle to overcome in seeking help. Learning to ask for and accept assistance from trained medical professionals, educators, and others is a huge step toward healing. Since I have been diagnosed I have found plenty of websites, support groups, and books that offer insight and assistance for people in the same boat as I am. Knowing you are not alone is a huge relief in itself! I also highly suggest a therapist specializing in the treatment of ADD/HD.

What follows is my account of my life so far, many of my experiences growing up with undiagnosed ADD, and how I cope with the symptoms of ADD as an adult. Finally being diagnosed with ADD has given me a liberating explanation of my past and confidence in my success in the future. Life has just begun!

Let's walk together, you and me.

1

What is ADD/HD

ADD is Attention Deficit Disorder, and ADHD is Attention Deficit Hyperactive Disorder. ADD is a neurobiological mental disorder, which causes a difficulty in focusing, concentrating, distractibility, and forgetfulness. Individuals with ADHD deal with those symptoms and added issues of hyperactivity and restlessness. ADD/HD can cause severe difficulty in learning and doing ordinary activities. Those of us afflicted with this disorder tend to be easily distracted by inner thoughts and things going on around us, and have very short attention spans. Individuals with ADD/HD usually have a history of problems with school, work, and relationships. Millions of adults and children have been diagnosed with ADD/HD and it is estimated that there are millions more who remain undiagnosed and suffering. ADD/HD can be treated, and many people go on to lead successful lives, even abundantly successful.

ADD is perceived by many as a disadvantage. If left undiagnosed, it certainly can be a difficulty for both the person with the disorder and the people surrounding him or her. It can be frustrating, devastating, and demoralizing. Surprisingly, having ADD can also be extremely beneficial to those who have it. Diagnosed ADD can help reveal and unlock amazing abilities within a person, helping them overcome other hardships. I have been told that people with ADD are similar to comic book heroes who have superpowers. I can see how that connection can be made. Many comic book heroes are outcasts and, like those with ADD, are different and have special talents not easily explained. My talents give me major advantages which have helped me to become successful and learn to balance my weaknesses with my strengths. With ADD, writing this book may be difficult, but I want to do it; and hopefully, accomplishing this, I might help and give hope to others.

This book is not a replacement for medical advice or assistance. It is the story of my life and my opinions, and it is my sincerest effort to help both you and me. I have ADD. I may have had ADHD at one time, but now I only have ADD. The reason I say that now I only have ADD and might have been ADHD is that my father beat the H (hyperactive) part out of me at a very young age. Unfortunately, my father was not able to beat out of me the rest of those letters. Of course, my father never knew I had ADD, so he considered me as either dumb or very lazy or both. He told me this countless times as I lay over my bed, waiting to be spanked for something I forgot or did not do. Sometimes it was for seemingly ignoring something he or my mother asked me to do. My father punished me a lot.

As I got older, and seemingly more dumb and lazy, my father's anger toward me increased and my punishments became more severe. My mother did not agree with my father's treatment of me for my behavior, but she was convinced that I was just lazy and didn't care about certain things. She noticed that when I was interested in something, I could concentrate for hours on end and accomplish things better than others could. My mother could not stop my father from physically disciplining me; he was a big man and rough around the edges. Finally, though, my mother did put her foot down and swore to leave him if he ever severely punished me again. He took her seriously and finally stopped, but I was already about fifteen years old at that time and had suffered through years of torment. The good thing about ADD is that I never focused on what happened to me for too long; in fact, I tended to forget most of it for long periods.

It was only recently, a year ago, at thirty-seven years of age, that I was diagnosed with ADD. In a very real way, the diagnosis of ADD helped me find myself and gain a better understanding of why I was the way I was as a child, as well as the way I am now. There was finally an explanation! I began to realize that there was a reason for my particular behaviors throughout my life. For the first time in thirty-seven years, I had hope. The symptoms of ADD described me so accurately. Here are just a few of the things I identified with instantly:

- Feeling easily distracted
- Inability to focus when needed
- Involuntarily hyper-focusing when not needed
- Difficulty finishing tasks
- Chronic issues with tardiness
- Forgetfulness
- Procrastination
- Impulsive behavior
- Depression
- Low self-esteem

The list goes on and on, and over the course of this story of my life you will read about how some of these symptoms affected me. Here is another list of what can be considered positive traits of someone with ADD. I will do my best to explain how these traits and talents have helped me and given me an advantage:

- Learning via osmosis (assimilation)
- Ability to multi task
- Dynamic
- Creative
- Vibrant
- Entertaining
- Compelling
- Imaginative
- Inventive
- Insightful
- Ability to hyper focus
- Resilient

I had heard of ADD before I had been diagnosed with it, but until then I never really paid much attention to what it was. I had read that it was a children's disorder and so I didn't make any connection to myself. I did not pay any attention to it – which is indeed a symptom of ADD. I grew up believing what my parents had persistently told me, that I was simply lazy and only chose the things in which I was interested. It made sense because whenever I became interested in something I could hyper focus on it and become an expert. Hyper focusing is indeed another familiar symptom of ADD. With respect to ADD/HD, hyper focusing is the ability to concentrate on something so intensely that one becomes so completely absorbed in a subject or activity that they can easily forget the time and their responsibilities.

The biggest problem of exhibiting some of the symptoms of ADD is that others misread them as my being unmotivated, rebellious, or unintelligent. I blamed myself for my perceived shortcomings for most of my life. As a kid, I wanted desperately to be a good person, do well in school, and make my parents proud. I tried to improve, and the harder I tried and failed, the more disappointed I became. This fear of failure made me feel depressed and isolated for most of my childhood. I was scared to come home with my report card. At times, I was scared to come home at all. When I was at home, I was very quiet and stayed in my room as much as possible. Sometimes I wished I could be forgotten or maybe I could run away and become a hermit, somewhere in the mountains. I always came home frightened because I never knew when the school might have called, or if I had forgotten to do something. If either of those things happened, I would be punished. Sometimes my punishment was to be grounded to my room, which was the punishment I prayed for most. For a very long time I hated the way I was and wished I could be someone else: a good kid, who did exactly what he was told to do. I couldn't change no matter how desperately I tried. I think my father believed I was doing it on purpose to make him angry, but making him angry was the last thing I wanted to do. I not only wanted my father to be proud of me, but I also wanted to be proud of myself. When I was growing up it did not seem as though I could succeed at either.

2

Ability to Achieve

Some people believe that having ADD/HD is a block that prevents adults and children from learning and performing as well as others. That simply is not true; ADDers simply learn differently, and thankfully, today more attention is placed on identifying learning disorders and helping adults and children through the learning process with consideration of ADD/HD. People with ADD/HD can indeed learn successfully with proper guidance and understanding. We ADDers are often gifted with very creative minds and we tend to have high I.Q.s. Our minds are constantly thinking and dreaming of creative ways to solve problems, taking in everything around us, and with that knowledge, finding new ways of doing things.

There are numerous people from history who are considered to have had ADD/HD: Alexander Graham Bell, Beethoven, Agatha Christie, Winston Churchill, Leonardo da Vinci, Walt Disney, Albert Einstein, and Abraham Lincoln, to name a few. Some well-known contemporaries reported to have ADD/HD include Jay Leno, Richard Branson, Charles Schwab, Whoopi Goldberg, Ty Pennington, and Paris Hilton. The list could go on, and I am sure if you were to research further, you would be amazed at how many fascinating, successful people have had or have ADD/HD.

I had already finished writing before adding Paris Hilton's name to this list of accomplished people with ADD/HD. She is a world famous celebrity and lives on a different level of society than most people. It is very interesting to me how her ADD symptoms are so obvious and yet still so misunderstood. The most fascinating thing about Ms. Hilton is how people respond to her. It seems that many people love to hate her and believe that she is a very fortunate and irresponsible person of wealth. Something, which seems to be stated quite frequently on the internet blogs and even in some news, is that Ms. Hilton does not deserve her attention and nobody seems to understand why she attracts so much of it. I consider Ms. Hilton to be extremely successful, brilliant, and a sensitive and kind person. ADD is a part of her brilliance. Within her world, she draws attention unlike any other. There are many people who are more successful and wealthier who haven't achieved her level of fame. I do not believe Ms. Hilton even tries to be famous. It is a part of her innate ADD nature. It's interesting to me that people are quick to criticize her for having so few accomplishments, and ignore the fact she is a world-renowned model, TV-Star, movie star, and bestselling author. The most fascinating thing about Ms. Hilton is the fact that no matter what her critics claim or even believe, they cannot stop paying attention to her. She has a dynamic personality and an allure all her own, like many ADDers are known to have.

In the past, it was common for people to reject others because of their mental or physical differences, especially when those differences are so misunderstood. For example, society has tried to get left-handed people to change the way they are for years. There is still a strong belief that lefties should learn to write with their right hand so they can fit in better and be more like everyone else. Most tools are created for righties only, making them difficult for lefties to use. Way back in the early part of the twentieth century, Roman Catholic Nuns would whack a leftie on the hand if he was caught trying to write the way it came naturally. This was in U.S. schools, by the way. Even in the 80's, children were frowned upon in schools if they had a natural inclination to write with their left hand. Some even considered lefties to have dealings with Satan. We might understand that certain aspects of treating a lefty differently are ridiculous and even border on ludicrous, but it doesn't change the fact that society has always wanted to change certain people because they seemed different in some way. Left-handed people are just as capable of writing and doing anything a right-handed person can do. The only time lefties are really inhibited is when certain things that they may use with their hands are made only for righties. Thankfully, that has changed dramatically in recent years. Now there is a decent amount of items made especially for lefties, like golf clubs, baseball mitts, computer mice, weapons holsters, and musical instruments. Unfortunately, it wasn't always this way. So with respect to handheld items being made for righties only, did that imply that being a lefty indicated a handicap? No, it means companies of mostly right-handers creating tools did not manufacture products with left-handers in mind. Sometimes people in our society can be unforgiving, particularly when they don´t understand why certain individuals are different from them.

On several occasions, it brought my mother to tears that she could not change me or get me to do certain things. It was so very painful to watch her in tears pleading with me to do something. It was upsetting to her when I wouldn't do as I was told, and she complained that I wanted to be physically punished because that was the only way I would obey. It can be extremely exasperating for a parent of an ADD/HD child to get the child to do simple chores. My mother tried her best to get me to do ordinary, expected things, such as do my homework, clean my room, walk the dog, or simply pay attention when someone spoke to me. When I would not comply, she would put me in a corner until I did comply, or my father would take matters into his own hands to make me comply. She would ask me countless times if I wanted to obey her or stand in a corner. I would stand there facing her unable to say a thing. I was frozen until she ordered me to stand in the corner. Today I understand why I always chose to stand in the corner. My imagination and creative mind always kept me occupied, whether I was lying in bed, sitting in school, or standing in a corner. Standing in a corner was a relief of sorts. It would give me time to be left alone, while appearing as though I was being punished. The fact of the matter is when it came to doing chores, I could not simply say yes and go do them. It is that simple and that complicated. It was not that I chose not to do them as my parents believed. I just couldn't. My brain would lock. My mind could not understand why I needed to do the chores or how. Yes, on the surface, I could understand the why, but my mind would go into hyper drive and ask so many questions that it left me immobile. Before I would ever start any task, I would already be exhausted from thinking about it. What's worse is that I could never figure out where to begin with a task and would spend precious time just standing there wondering. I would lift my hands to my hair and just pull in frustration. By going to the corner, I would avoid all of that. Just the mention of doing something physical, which involved any organization or structure, drove me crazy. When I chose to stand in the corner and not do something she had asked, my mother would become extremely frustrated with me. My behavior must have been so confusing to her.

The problem was that punishment was being used to correct my behavior. She was trying to be lenient with the type of punishment she proposed and used, but even so, it did not work. My mother's punishment was her way of protecting me from more severe punishment from my father by allowing me to choose to behave. It didn't work, so punishment from my father was unavoidable. When it came to getting me to do things such as chores, my father's punishment was usually very effective. When my father punished me, or just scared me out of my mind by threatening severe punishment, I found myself moving into action. My mind would unlock, focus, and I would start doing my chores. Punishment from my father was a powerful form of stimulation as it produced an adrenaline rush in me. Knowing what ADD/HD is and how it is treated, I understand now why my father's punishments worked. Most medications prescribed for people with ADD/HD are stimulants, which actually help calm the mind for focus, clarity, and direction. Adrenaline, a natural stimulant, can calm a person's mind and help them mentally focus for short periods. However, just as one dose of stimulating medication for a person with ADD/HD would not be an effective treatment, unpredictable rushes of adrenaline would also not be an effective way to modify behavior. My parents were astounded that I could be punished so much and still not choose to change my ways.

Today I have found several ways to stimulate my mind without pain and suffering. I take ginseng to help me focus and have clarity. Short but fast runs, as well as deep breathing exercises, help me focus my mind. On occasion, I drink a strong cup of coffee and the caffeine does the trick. I haven't grown out of my symptoms; I have simply found effective ways to cope with them. Mostly I put myself in situations where my strengths are used more. I do not believe punishment is the ultimate answer for the behavior problems ADDers have. It did not fix me as a child and it would not fix me today.

Another thing that helped me when I was younger was positive redirection. I did not understand what it was at the time, but I discovered it when visiting a friend of mine, named Matt, when I was around 16 years old. We were not very close friends, but we hung out every so often. Matt was an affable person, who seemed to be a neat freak because his room was always in such perfect order. Every other week when I had come over to visit, his room was changed around. It was always so interesting to be in his room and see how he had changed things. The bed would be on the other side of the room where his cabinet had been, his cabinet was against another wall, and even his posters had been changed or moved. The designs he came up with were so interesting that each time I visited I would need about a half an hour to take in all the changes. One time when I had visited Matt, his room was a mess. I asked him what had happened. He told me that his room usually became a mess, but that I typically came over after he had just redesigned it. He said that he usually redesigned his room once a week. While I was there his mother came in and asked Matt when he would get around to redesigning the room. She did not ask him when he was going to clean his room, but instead asked him specifically when he would be redesigning his room. They looked around the room together, discussed some ideas, and even asked me for my input. Then she left. Matt did not start making any changes to his room while I was there; we went outside and goofed off instead. He wasn't put in the corner or spanked, and no one had come after him to attend to his room right away. I came over again two days later and his room was in impeccable condition. His room was changed and completely awesome. He had even hung some new posters, creating a cool new theme. Finally, I had asked him if someone was doing this for him or if he was doing it himself. He told me that he always did it himself, but that his mother and father often had suggestions. I became so intrigued by his interesting room designs that I decided that I wanted to redesign my own room. When I went home that evening, I started redesigning my own room. First, I had to clean my room, but that was okay because I was so motivated and focused on designing it, that it did not seem like a meaningless chore. I received such positive reviews from my sisters and parents that I began redesigning my room once a week. From then on, I rarely ever needed to be told to clean my room again.

I now realize that Matt's mother used positive redirection as a way to get Matt to do certain things without ever resorting to punishments. Most kids do not like cleaning up their rooms; they would rather be playing and having fun. By having Matt redesign his room, she had given him something fun and interesting to do while at the same time accomplishing the ultimate goal of getting the room clean. Matt's mother understood him well and knew how to motivate him by using positive redirection. If parents take the time to get to know their children, their interests, and their particular needs, they can more effectively communicate with them. Children with ADD/HD especially need positive communication and positive reinforcement from their parents and teachers in order to thrive.

3

Education

Okay, in true ADDer fashion I have gotten a little ahead of myself. I am going to back up a little. I only have a few memories of my life before I started school. I was born in California, the son of an enlisted US Air Force Sergeant. My mother is from Holland, where my father had met her, and where my older sister was born. Being in the military, you would think that we traveled a lot. We did move a few times, but far fewer times than the average military family. My father had been re-assigned to Germany when I was 7 years old. I have lived in Germany ever since. Most of my formal education was in Germany at U.S. Department of Defense Schools.

My father and mother eventually took me out of school when I was sixteen, in tenth grade. They felt that the cost of the tuition for school was not worth it if I refused to take it seriously and get good grades. I understood their reasons at the time because I rarely earned any grades above a D. To this day, I do not understand how I passed each year of school, moving on to the next level, when my grades were always so poor. The only grade I had to repeat was the first grade.

My first troubles began when I started preschool. I did not like school because it was very boring to me. I didn't understand why I had to be there and spent most of my days daydreaming until I could go home. Trying to get me involved in class must have been extremely difficult for my teachers. I don't remember doing much in class other than staring out the window and dreaming. I don't know what I dreamed about at that age (the exciting daydreams would come later). I also don't remember getting in too much trouble with my parents during preschool. The next year, when grades would begin to mean something, the real trouble would start.

First grade was shocking, the end of my thus, so far, blessed life. I learned nothing during my first year of school, I did not pay attention at all, and to this day, I have no idea what my teacher's name was. I don't remember how my parents reacted to my first report cards; however I do remember the way my father reacted after the last day of school when I tried to hide my school notebook which contained my final grade. I was afraid that I was going to be in trouble for my grades. Instead of taking my notebook home with me, I went out onto the playground and hid it there. Therefore, even being that young, I must have had some feelings of fear and guilt that I was not measuring up academically. I did not hide my notebook very well because the very next day after playing outside, I walked in the door and my father had it in his hands. I do not remember what my father said, I only remember his hand slapping me across the face and him asking me why I tried to hide my notebook. I was sent to my room crying and confused. Already, by the end of first grade, my father was angry and disappointed with me. Throughout my days in school my father would never stop being angry and unhappy with me. I had to repeat first grade, and somehow I made it through that year and made it to second grade.

It was between first and second grade that we moved to Germany with a new addition to our family. I now had a little sister to go along with my older sister. In second grade I was put into a special education class for learning how to read and write. I did very well in that class, surpassing all expectations. Because of how well I did in the special education class, I was soon re-assigned to a regular level class again. While in the special education class, I was with only a handful of other students, so the student to teacher ratio was small. I remember that special education class was interesting and fun and I interacted closely with the teacher. That class was by far my best learning experience in school. It didn't take long for me to start losing interest in school again when I returned to the regular second grade level. I was back in a class with thirty other students and I could get away with daydreaming for the most part. It was embarrassing to be called upon during class to answer a question though, because I usually had no idea what the teacher was talking about. Inability to pay attention is a significant symptom of ADD. Often throughout my years of school I would be called upon to answer questions and participate orally in class, but most of the time I was off somewhere in a daydream. It was so embarrassing and humiliating. My teachers would give me a pathetic look or say something degrading to me, and I could hear the other student in the classes snickering at me. Many teachers thought I did not pay attention on purpose, as if I was bored with them and the class. I was bored, but not on purpose. I tried to pay attention and do well in school, but I rarely ever accomplished either. I would try to do well and focus on the lessons, but before I realized it, I was off in a daydream world and I didn't even realize I had gone there. It seemed as if someone else controlled my thoughts and my brain. Already, from the beginning of my formal education, I found it difficult to concentrate on my assignments and get through a school day without daydreaming in class.

During the summer between second and third grades, my family and I had gone on a trip to Holland to visit my grandparents and cousins. I enjoyed going on long scenic road trips to Holland because it was an opportunity for me to simply stare out the car window and let my imagination flow freely. Usually when we visited our relatives, my parents were always busy and didn't really pay any attention to me. I had so much unstructured free time that I could daydream uninterrupted. That was a real treat.

During one of these five-hour trips to Holland, I imagined that I was a leader of a group of superheroes with incredible super powers who traveled the galaxy in an awesome spaceship. Our mission was to seek out evil doers and vanquish them. Over the weeks and months that I daydreamed about my hero and his group, I started to give them names. My superhero's name became Commander Mart, the leader of the Silver Eagles. Commander Mart and the Silver Eagles was my favorite thing to think about at the time. However, most of the time, my imagination was hard to control. When I tried to imagine something specific, many other thoughts or images would overwhelm my mind. I found it difficult for me to focus my mind on a specific daydream when I wanted to. I could understand having no control over my dreams while sleeping, but feeling that I had no control over my daydreams while I was awake was frustrating. I enjoyed daydreaming about Commander Mart and the Silver Eagles and because of that, I wanted to learn how to find a way to control my thoughts. Imagining those characters and their adventures through space was so intriguing to me that I forced myself to focus on that specific story in my mind. This was the first time I learned on my own to focus my own thoughts on a specific idea that was particularly very exciting and interesting to me.

As I entered third grade I started to realize that I was not like other kids. I did not know why I was different, and I began to believe that maybe I wasn't as smart as they were. I was ridiculed in class by students and teachers for not answering questions correctly or paying attention, and then I would go home and be in trouble by my parents for not being smarter or better in school. The other kids knew answers and turned in their assignments on time. They received praise, smiley face stickers, and gold stars. I was just there, always in trouble for not doing what I was supposed to. I felt ashamed to be me, and I would try to do as well as them, but I didn't know how. I wanted to be like the other kids. I assumed everyone probably daydreamed as I did, but I was the one who was not able to be successful at school. I began to feel dumb and lonely and looked for ways to escape those feelings. I would usually escape into my own imagination, where I could create my own world of wonderful superheroes and their amazing adventures. It was the easy and natural thing for me to do.

Things improved for me a little bit when I met a very special person in an unusual way. Up until then I had been pretty much a loner and then, unexpectedly, that changed on the playground. During lunch recess one day, a kid jumped me from behind and started to beat me up. Dirt was everywhere: in my mouth, in my eyes, and down my pants. One minute he was on top of me, landing a fist against my cheek and the next minute I was on top of him, swinging my fists wildly. It was my first fight, and this kid was kicking my butt. To this day, I have no idea why we fought. I don't think we really knew each other before our fight on the playground, but we may have talked before and disagreed about something. To my relief, the recess bell ended our fight and we stopped as the crowd around us started to disperse. A strange thing happened after that. This kid, who happened to be new to the school, offered me his hand and helped me get up. Dumbstruck, and not wanting to be hit again, I took his hand and got up. That is how I met Phil. Phil had a magnetic personality and an exciting energy about him that drew me to him instantly. He was easily likable and I thought he was a very cool kid.

Even though my first memory of Phil was our fighting, we went on to become best friends for several years. Phil was my first friend in school and the thing that he liked most about me was that I liked being around him and that I went along with his adventures. In our own individual ways, we were different from other kids. Even though we were not as smart in the classroom, we could just about outwit anyone outside of the classroom. We even outsmarted adults at times. Phil was a brave person who dared to do things that I wouldn't dare to do because I feared my father's harsh punishment for any trouble I could have gotten into. I was the innocent looking onlooker that got us out of countless messes with neighbors, teachers, and his parents.

When I look back on things knowing now that I have ADD, I can understand why I was drawn to Phil's friendship and not that of others. Phil was a highly stimulating person, and he always had something exciting to say and do. Phil had problems of his own and I guess he was drawn to my friendship because, like me, he just didn't fit in with others. He was popular, but he did not get into the popularity thing. It was through my friendship with Phil that I discovered I had talents. With him, I learned so many new things about the world and myself. Most importantly, he helped me realize that I was not a complete loser and that I had value as a person.

Elementary school went by as if it were a dream and sometimes a nightmare. Seventh grade, junior high, was a completely new experience for me. There were multiple classrooms, and I was used to spending the school day in one classroom with one teacher and one group of students. I felt a little lost and overwhelmed having to change classes all day with different people in every one. It was scary, but I was also excited about the new experience. After the first day, I was already overwhelmed. There were so many new people to meet and so many new teachers to understand and try to obey. In each class, I found a seat near the back to try to be anonymous. The back of the class is the worst place for an ADDer to be. During middle school, I learned the art of being quiet and unassuming. The classes were full of other students and rarely did the teachers seem to care what I did as long as I remained quiet and respectful. There were one or two teachers who cared about me and tried to reach out, but the majority of them didn't care who I was, what my learning problems may have been, or if I would succeed in the future. I daydreamed more and paid attention less in middle and high school. I often remember teachers just placing my graded tests on my desk without as much as a word. An F or a D would be written next to my name at the top of the paper, but that's about as much personal communication I received from my teachers. Receiving bad grades only became painful when my report card was sent home. I would be punished at home for my grades, but I was not able to make any significant changes at school. I continued to daydream and pay no real attention to anything that was being taught.

I do remember having one teacher in particular who seemed to care about my academic success. Her name was Ms. Holland and she was one of my ninth grade teachers. She surprised me really. I sat at the back of her class as I had done in all my other classes, but she just wouldn't ignore me. She tried to figure me out. She talked to me on a regular basis and frequently told me that I could do better. She wasn't always nice about it though. After a while, I wanted her to leave me alone. Moreover, when she gave me a failing grade, I took it personally. I was failing in all of my other classes, and yet I took her grade personally. She had inspired me at first to do better in her class and that was what started to annoy me. I became annoyed because I tried to do better and she kept devaluing my best efforts. I would go home and repeatedly read the chapters that she had assigned, but the next day when she would ask me about them, I just couldn't remember what I had read at the time she would ask. Remembering and understanding what I had read would only come to me days later — never right away or predictably. By the time what I had read started to surface in my mind, she only believed that I had finally decided to read the chapters and therefore I was in some way just playing with her. Unfortunately, I became the center of attention in that class as Ms. Holland proceeded to make an example out of me by openly ridiculing me. I couldn't believe it. I was trying to do as I had always done and just sit unassumingly in the back of the class. Once, she sat me in the hall to take a test. The rest of the class took the test in the class. It was not an open book test, but Ms. Holland gave me the book and allowed me to look up the answers. I still failed that test. It didn't matter that she had given me the book. I sat in the hall alone, and nobody was observing whether I was taking the test or not. I don't think I even opened the book. I was so upset during that test that all I did was concentrate on being placed in the hall. Before I knew it, the class was over and I hadn't answered a single question. When Ms. Holland collected my test, she looked at it and then looked back at me with dismay. She had asked me why I didn't study for her class or care about it. I simply told her that I didn't know. I didn't bother to tell her that I did try to study and that I did read the chapters, because I figured she would not believe me. She told me that she thought I was a bright kid and that perhaps I should start to take school more seriously. Usually, a week or two after she gave me a reading assignment I would come back and give her a detailed oral report of the chapters that had been assigned in an effort to show that I was trying. She would not give me a grade for these reports or even seriously consider them, but she must have realized that I knew and understood everything that I had read. She did not understand or believe that I found it difficult to put together certain information in my mind in the time required. Ms. Holland did not realize or take into consideration that I learned differently from most of her other students.

Generally, that's the way school was for me. Most of my teachers probably thought that I did not try hard enough to succeed. I felt that none of the teachers understood me, because they were too busy trying to teach me in a way that was right for them, but impossible for me. It was tough getting through my school years feeling misunderstood by my teachers and with the belief that I must be stupid.

Once I was out of high school and away from standardized rules, I found my own way of learning. I believe that if had had more teachers like my second grade special education teacher, I might not have performed so poorly in school. She paid attention to my educational needs in the way that I needed them. She listened to me, observed my abilities and limitations, and then educated me in a way that worked for me. It is the only time in school that I remember excelling for the full duration of the lessons. The special education teacher thought very well of me, and mentioned to me that I might have an attention disorder because I had difficulty learning on my own. Back then, in the mid to late 70's, ADD was not well known and not considered seriously as a learning disorder. People considered it more as an excuse for bad behavior than a learning disorder. I am not sure what my parents determined from my academic success in that special class, but I think that's when they decided I was lazy. The following year I was put back into a regular class and I never completely passed a class again. I can only imagine where I would be today if my parents had considered that maybe, just maybe, I was not lazy and that my learning problems were beyond my control. There were also times that my mother hired a personal tutor for me. In the fifth grade specifically, I remember Mrs. Adams was my tutor. She lived next door and helped me with my homework. Her tutoring helped me do well in my fifth grade class. That proved right there that I could do it; however, I needed some help. The personal direction and guidance I received from my second grade teacher and my tutor helped me to succeed academically when I could not on my own. But by that time, my parents firmly believed that I was just lazy. I think that my doing well with the help of a tutor proved to them I was lazy, because yes, I could succeed, but obviously not if left up to my own devices. Many children with undiagnosed ADD/HD don't have the best educational experience, because they are mistakenly considered by parents and educators as lazy and uninterested in school. Some educators and even parents believe that ADD/HD is a myth.

ADD/HD is not a modern myth, as some skeptics would like us to believe. ADD/HD is a very real neurobiological condition recognized by the American Medical Association, the U.S. Surgeon General, and the American Psychological Association. It is also recognized as a medical condition under the Americans with Disabilities Act of 1990. Medical experts agree that ADD/HD is a legitimate medical condition, which manifests in ways that can be difficult to manage without proper diagnosis and treatment. ADD/HD is not even a new disorder. One of the first stories written about a child with ADD/HD is *Fidgety Philip*, written by a German physician Heinrich Hoffman in 1848. British pediatrician, George Frederic Still, was already conducting research concerning ADD/HD in children in 1902.

It is the responsibility of educators and parents to be aware that not all children learn in the same way and that there might be something more to be considered with a child other than just laziness or lack of intelligence.

4

Interests & Distractions

People with Attention Deficit Disorder, or ADDers, love television, movies, comic books and other visually and mentally captivating media. As a child, I absorbed and processed a lot of useful information by reading a lot, watching movies and TV, and daydreaming. One could say that all kids love those things, and that those things are a problem because they are considered a distraction for most people. However, ADDers hyper focus on things that are interesting to us and that stimulate our creative minds. Not only do we absorb the information, we automatically analyze it and cross-reference it with what we already know as we process it in our minds. This happens below the surface and we do not even realize it is happening. ADDers always seem to be lost in thought, because they take in so much information that in order for it to make sense they have to process it in a way that works best for them. What I have come to understand about my own daydreaming is that I am often analyzing information and putting it together in a way that *my* mind understands it. It's actually a creative process of learning in the form of story daydreams.

I explained to my mother recently how having ADD affected my childhood and my education. She told me that she thought I did well in elementary school and that it was in seventh grade when I started to have serious problems. I have thought about what she meant and I can see why she thought that. ADDers are good fakers and we do what we can to get by. ADDers have a hard time conforming to the structure of the traditional education system without medication and treatment. What we do is find ways to get by and find ways to stay out of trouble with our parents and teachers. It didn't always work for me, though. Kids with ADD/HD must survive in a structured world of rules, which are not designed for them. When I was growing up with undiagnosed ADD in the 70's and 80's, I had to learn survival skills to get by without punishment. Today ADD/HD is better understood by doctors, teachers, and parents, therefore early diagnosis and treatment is more often available to children earlier in their educational and social development.

ADDers can be very intelligent. Many people believe Einstein may have had ADD/HD. People with ADD/HD have the ability to learn a great deal of complex information; however, as I explained, we tend to learn in untraditional ways. Thanks to our ability to hyper focus we can become experts in just about anything that interests us. Attaining college degrees may not be terribly easy for us, but if we have chosen to learn something on our own, we can become extremely adept at it. We are able to subconsciously analyze and understand complicated concepts, and even devise innovative new ideas. In the fifth grade, I hyper focused on my science class because I found the subject particularly interesting that year. I received the highest grade in my class in science that year, and barely passed any of the other subjects. The next year I lost interest in science and did not do nearly as well in it. My inconsistent performance in school was frustrating for me, and especially my teachers.

The most frustrating thing for me was my inability to stay interested in things I liked doing for very long. In sixth grade, I talked my father into getting me a guitar. For the first six months, I was so engrossed in my guitar that I learned quickly how to play it well. I was enrolled in a guitar class, and I did so well the first few months that the teacher put me in his advanced class. After about a month in the advanced guitar class, I began to lose interest in playing and before I knew it, my interest had moved on to something else. I moved on to martial arts. I watched all of Bruce Lee's movies and wanted to become a famous martial artist. My father signed me up for a karate class and within a few short weeks, the instructor hailed me a natural. Once again, I did so well that I was promoted several levels within the span of just a few months. I felt good while I was practicing martial arts, but I lost interest in that too. Bicycling and skateboarding were very enjoyable to me and I did those things for a while as well. As difficult as it was to focus on schoolwork, I found it nearly as difficult to focus long term on my hobbies.

ADDers tend to lose interest in things that require daily mundane practice and give up on them easily. We like the excitement of learning something quickly and proficiently and being the best at something new. When I did well in that first guitar class, I was elated and felt very good about myself. I used all my effort to be the best in the class because I enjoyed the positive feedback I received. However, when I was put into the advanced guitar class I felt incompetent compared to the other students in that class, who were far more musically developed than I was. Situations like this made me feel depressed and enhanced my already low self-esteem. I just couldn't imagine practicing everyday to improve slowly over time. I did not have the patience to focus on the daily task of practicing what I had already learned and catch up to the other classmates. Without the intense stimulation of learning something new and the rewards of being the best, I lost interest quickly. I felt badly about this, but I had no idea what to do.

I also quit my martial arts training, but for different reasons. From the start, I was a natural at karate and I showed a lot of potential. I quickly advanced from belt to belt. I was great at forms and maneuvers, but I did not do well sparring with my classmates. I was afraid to fight back during the sparring matches in class. The way I fought wildly with Phil in the third grade was not in me anymore. When I began learning karate, I was in tenth grade. By that time I had experienced years of my father's angry outbursts toward me, and I had become passive and afraid to fight back. I had been beaten down mentally so much over the years that I felt powerless to fight back, even in a controlled sparring match with gloves. I was laughed at and ridiculed during any sparring matches that I did participate in, so I walked away from karate too. Giving up karate was not a direct result of my learning disorder; it was because of the severe punishments I had received from my father and how they affected me.

This issue I had with not fighting back and trying to avoid conflict almost cost me my life one day. My father encouraged me to take the martial arts classes because he wanted me to be tough and learn a fighting skill so that I could defend myself. I don't think he understood that years of his harsh punishments and living with his anger towards me was frightening and had affected me negatively for a long time. Even years after I had moved out of my parents' house, I flinched at sudden movements that people made. One day when I was downtown, I flinched around the wrong person. We were having a good time at first, until a topic of discussion came up which angered him. He wanted to know why I hadn't stayed in touch or seem to care about anybody. He had mistaken my distracted nature for arrogance and pompousness. He was in an agitated state. The more agitated and loud he got, the more my discomfort showed. He started making sudden movements toward me, as if to hit me, and I instinctively flinched. I don't believe he would have tried anything further if I had not flinched. He knew that I had taken martial arts classes and he had seen me demonstrate kicks and moves, but never seen me actually fight. My nervousness seemed to enrage him, and before I knew it, he hit me across the face as hard as he could. I went down and my whole body started to shake. While I was on the ground, he started kicking me with all of his force. I nearly died that day. Had the police not arrived in time, I might not have made it. My leg had been broken and my face and body looked like ground meat. Blood was everywhere. I hardly felt the pain. All I could do was wish for the beating to stop. It took months for me to heal and during that time I rested and recovered on my parents' sofa. My father would sit with me and explain to me that I needed to learn to fight back and he gave me some handgrips to strengthen my hands. I did not bother to explain to him that I was beaten because I was unable to fight back. It had absolutely nothing to do with my physical abilities. He never seemed to have understood. Any time I tried to express my concerns to my parents, they would dismiss me and say that I was looking for excuses for my inaction and that I did not know what I was talking about. Talking to them was difficult because they never considered my concerns or problems relevant or valid. My parents had always told me what I was about and what motivated me. I could have died that day and it had nothing to do with any lack of understanding of how to fight back. It was because of my inner fear to fight back.

Another typical trait of ADDers is to be forgetful and lose things that are important to us. When I turned fourteen, my mother bought me a fantastic skateboard. She had found it in a shop in Holland and it was not just some plastic piece with wheels on it. It had fat wheels, a fat wooden board with sandpaper to keep my feet from slipping. I treasured that skateboard, and it took me all over our town. It was the best skateboard around. In the mid eighties in Germany, skateboards like mine were a hot commodity and hard to find. I had many offers from other kids to buy my board, but I turned every one of them down. I didn`t want to give that board up for anything. Unfortunately though, I lost my favorite skateboard because I had left it at a friend`s house and forgotten to go get it. I used to ride it between my town and the next town where Phil and other friends lived. There was a wonderful downhill stretch between our towns that was a lot of fun sailing down, but was no fun going back up. Whenever I arrived at a friend's house riding my board, I would usually find a good place outside to hide it. I did that because I didn't want to struggle riding the board back up the hill. Often I would get a ride home either from my friend's parents or one of my parents would pick me up. Just about every time, I would forget to get my board and bring it home with me. Sometimes my board would stay for days in the place I had hidden it. Even though I loved it so much, I never felt any urgency to retrieve it. Eventually, I had waited too long to get my skateboard from where I had hidden it, and it was gone forever. Although I was upset, I was not surprised.

I lost my all time favorite bike in a similar way. When I was sixteen, my father bought me a new bike. My father went through a lot of time and effort to help me pick out a nice bike when I was sixteen. Buying the bike was one of the nicest things that my father had ever done for me and you would think I would take much better care of it. That bike was an awesome ten-speed with a spectacular blue paint job. I constantly rode it back and forth between the towns, and just as I had done with my skateboard, I did with my bike. I usually left it in a narrow space between Phil's house and a wall. The bike was always out of sight and could stay there for days without being touched. However, one day when I went over to Phil's, I went into town with him and his mother and left my bike at his house. His mother dropped me off at my home later that day, and I hadn't returned for my bike. Although I still went over plenty of times to Phil's house by other means, I continued to leave my bike there for maybe three or four months. During that time, Phil and his family moved away. Even after Phil moved, I still had plenty of chances to pick up my bike and I just never did. I always considered that the laziest thing I ever did. Considering my actions, it seems that I did not care for the bike that much, but I sincerely did. As with many things in my life, I was able to leave it behind without much consideration. I loved that bike and rode it constantly for months on end and then one day it seemed like it didn't mean that much to me anymore and I just abandoned it. I never knew why I acted that way, and now with an ADD diagnosis, I see how easily my interests can change outside of my own control. Eventually the bike was gone and when I noticed it was gone, I was heartbroken. I had no right to be upset and I blamed and degraded myself for being so irresponsible far longer than that bike had been a part in my life.

That is something important to remember about people with ADD/HD. No matter how angry someone can get at us for our seemingly irresponsible and neglectful actions, it is nothing compared to how angry or punishing we can be to ourselves for our actions. Although it seems we are doing self-defeating things on purpose, we are not. As much as a normal person cannot understand the total disregard we seem to have at times, it is not always within our control. It's rarely in our control without medication, behavioral therapy, or specialized coaching. We understand the difference between right and wrong, but it is just that sometimes we do not consider the implications or consequences of our actions or inactions. We can be extremely impulsive and neglectful.

Have you ever driven somewhere and, upon your arrival, you do not completely remember the route you took? It could be from daydreaming or thinking back over your hectic day. Well, that's a good example of how ADDers are on a regular basis. Our minds do not go blank, but we simply have so many different thoughts and considerations going through our heads that we lose track very easily.

I do not believe in the myth that we grow out of ADD/HD. I think many of us figure ourselves out better as we grow, and we learn to work with our type of thinking in order to get by. Knowing what we do and why we do it helps us compensate in various ways.

5

Reliving the Past

Living in the past, even as a youngster, is something ADDers do in order to feel good or boost our confidence, especially when things are not going so well in the present. For some reason, even though our short-term memories aren't that great, we can often call up memories, long past, as if we were still at that time and place. There probably is nothing wrong with our short-term memory. It is just that we are so constantly distracted by our thoughts that we do not always focus on what's going on around us in the here and now. Then when we come out of our daydreaming, we seem to be lost or confused and do not recollect what a teacher was saying or what we might have been reading or watching.

To make sense of what I mean concerning living in the past, you must first try to understand that sometimes people with ADD grow up feeling as if they are disappointing their parents, their teachers, and most everyone else around them. Not only do we disappoint our parents and friends, but also we are severely punished for our actions. Not all punishment is physical and for most people it comes in the verbal form – it doesn't matter how the punishment is given. The result is the same in creating a person with little or no self-esteem, tremendous self-doubt, and deep-seeded feelings of worthlessness. How would you feel if you were continuously punished because you have blue eyes and not brown? Just as no one chooses their eye color, ADDers do not chose to have a learning and attention disorder.

Considering that we ADDers are constantly in some kind of trouble, anytime we experience a good outcome or live through an enjoyable situation, we like to go back to that time and relive that success in our minds. That's recommended for just about anyone to feel better. To do it too much and always consider what could have been or what should have been is not healthy and can inhibit a person's personal development. Some people live with an endless wanting desire for what is no longer there, without moving forward in life. Most people, who do not have ADD, look upon the past and take away from it learning experiences and move on to the future a wiser and better person. Conversely, a person with ADD has difficulty capturing the lessons that should have been learned from their experiences and has a hard time moving forward toward new horizons. Additionally, such as in my case, that lack of learning from the past can contribute to being naïve.

The other side of living in the past is that often we ADDers cannot get over mistakes that we have made, things we have said or things we've done. We tend to relive these situations and severely beat ourselves up mentally for our failings. Obsessing over the past is a serious and distressing habit of ADDers and adds more complex difficulties to our already diminished psyche. I guess, in a way, I thought if I punished myself enough for my past mistakes and neglectful ways, I would stop and do better. To some degree, I did do a tad better for a short while and since this process had seemingly beneficial effects, I did it more and more. It was almost as if I believed that if I punished myself enough I would feel better, or beat into my brain never to make the same mistakes. ADDers repeat the same mistakes. We don't want to, of course, but we can't seem to help it. That has a lot to do with the opposite of hyper focusing, which is not focusing at all. By putting situations totally behind us, we allow ourselves to forget about it completely. I have since trained myself to examine and learn from situations and see them reasonably. However, by the time I realized how to do this and gain understanding from it, I had already missed many opportunities in my life.

It was much later, in my early twenties, when I started to discover that I was not exactly on par with my friends and coworkers in a social context. This discovery had little to do with my education and more to do with my everyday knowledge. I didn't know much about the world outside of my mind, and when I started living on my own, this lack of knowledge made me appear naïve and out of touch. I wore clothes that were mismatched and out of style, I had trouble sustaining relationships, and I had little idea of what I should do with the rest of my life. I did have wants and needs but I didn't have a clue how to go about achieving them.

ADD does have its good aspects, though. People with ADD can be, and often are, creative geniuses and talented in many areas. Regardless of how naïve we seem to be, we have a way of finding unusual ways to solve problems, and are probably the most talented at finding an unorthodox, but effective, way to do just about anything. It's quite normal for our ways to be unconventional and yet be very effective. I consider myself very successful in many areas of my life, even with a drawback such as ADD.

In ninth grade, my elective was a computer class. I failed it miserably, but it was entertaining and I enjoyed it. I look back upon it as a personal success. My poor teacher must have pulled her hair out trying to understand me. The thing is, somehow I used the knowledge in my brain to focus it in ways I did not yet understand. I could not figure out or remember normal assignments about computer commands and creating computer reports; however, the lessons on creative design stuck in my head and I focused on them intently – you could say I hyper focused on them. Each week we had quizzes about the things we had learned and I never could remember specific commands or other computer jargon so I would always fail the quizzes. On the other hand, I did quite well at graphic design. At the end of each quarter, the class had a contest for graphic creations of screensavers. Our teacher asked several of her colleagues to come into the class and judge the creations. The graphics that could be created in those days on a computer were not as elaborate as they are today and you had to type in certain commands for colors and movements. Somehow, I remembered those commands easily and I created some amazing designs. Each quarter I won the graphic competition and each time I could see my teacher shake her head in disbelief and wonder. I can understand today why I did what I did and how I did it. However, my teacher *never* once asked me how I did what I did or was even concerned that I could do it so well and still fail her class.

Keep in mind that we ADDers need high stimulus to become hyper focused and interested in just about anything, so as a result, when we create something that interests us it is usually very stimulating, especially for non ADDer minds. Therefore, our creations are considered outstanding and impressive to others without ADD. Think how much it takes to stimulate our ADD minds and you can start to understand why our creations are highly sought after. It is an amazing gift. I did not know this part of me was a gift until I was diagnosed with ADD and my therapist pointed it out to me. What was of further interest to me, and I did not realize, is that I did not trust my abilities, which is, of course, also typical of ADD/HD persons. The problem is complex and yet simple. Through much of my life, my ideas and concepts have been outright rejected, ignored, or scrutinized to the point I didn't even believe in them anymore.

It is a shame the computer teacher did not try to find out why I did so well in a certain area and so poorly in another. Didn't she recognize I had some talents? She was able to see a young man in action that didn't make any sense. I mean, how can someone not remember almost all other commands and yet remember those belonging to a certain assignment? I bet she thought I ignored the other things and only concentrated on what was fun and enjoyable. Yes, she was right if she thought that, but it wasn't by my choice. I wanted to do well in all aspects of the class but I simply could not get my mind to focus on the things I subconsciously considered boring.

A similarly disheartening thing happened to me when I was in a ninth grade electronics class. The class was designed for people who wanted to get a little ahead and do extra work. The class was assigned fifteen chapters in the textbook to be completed at our own pace, but by the end of the quarter. Well, I completed them well in advance of the deadline. That was great, but it was also problematic for me. I ended up having to wait for the rest of the class to catch up, and I became bored and disinterested while I waited. I asked my teacher, on several occasions, for extra assignments, but I was told to wait for the class to catch up and that I should have paced myself. When I look back now, I almost laugh at the thought ... ask an ADDer to pace himself? I waited for the rest of the class, but I needed to stay occupied while I waited. Therefore, I created several things that I had learned from the textbook and tried to present them to the teacher. He was nice and polite, but told me again that I would have to wait for the rest of the class to catch up and that we would have creative assignments in the following chapters. During the time I waited, I ended up frustrating the teacher and upsetting my fellow students. Some of them wanted to compete for who could do the most within the specified time and they didn't have a chance against my hyper focusing and ability to analyze things so quickly when hyper focused. It created conflict that I did not want. I was just doing what came natural to me, and people took offense to it. Even the teacher believed that I was competing and wanted to show the class up. I later found out that the teacher thought I already had education in electronics, but I never took electronics classes before, nor learned on my own, before this particular class. By the time the class caught up with me, I was bored out of my mind and had no interest whatsoever in continuing the class. I tried to stay interested and pace myself, but in reality I just didn't care about the class anymore. I knew if I started to care, I would end up in the same situation; with people upset with me. I ended up failing that class and never taking electronics again. Focusing on what interests me and ignoring the rest of the requirements in a structured setting was a problem for me repeatedly throughout my life. This type of problem had perplexed me beyond reason until I was diagnosed with ADD, and my therapist helped me realize exactly what was happening.

6

Common Sense

Something I have been credited with having as an adult is good common sense. No matter who you are, or where you are, the most beneficial trait you can have is good old-fashioned common sense. You might be thinking that people with ADD/HD or any learning disorder would not have good common sense, but that's just not true. I have met many people who are well educated who simply do not have good judgment, and that holds them back when they should be flourishing. As a manager, I have passed up numerous people for promotions simply because of common sense issues. Yes, I learned my job; however, there comes a point when you must be able to initiate common sense. You will find that most leaders have very good common sense and often the people whom they value the most are not necessarily the smartest people they have on board, but rather the people that have basic knowledge and an abundance of common sense.

I might not be as successful as I would like to be or think I should be, but I am successful in many areas of my life, to include my work. As I have mentioned, I did not do that well in school because it did not interest me. What did catch my attention were books, movies, magazines and many other forms of media. I read many novels by Stephen King, David Eddings and the like. In addition, I watched a lot of popcorn TV, and I loved the history channels. Maybe that's not getting a proper education, but it is what kept my attention. Attention is the key to ADD/HD people, obviously. If it catches their attention, watch out! An ADD/HD person is usually incredibly creative and has a lot of common sense, and can become an inventor, entrepreneur, or someone with revolutionary ideas in just about any area.

In the company where I work, for example, I have created things to be used for the purpose of email advertising and developing sales. Some of the things I have suggested and created are used in some form or another globally by the company. The funny thing is, I started my employment history as a pizza driver and have made my way up to being a respected manager and public affairs representative for my company. This speaks highly of the upward mobility our company offers and its ability to see potential in its employees. Remember, I am a person who was removed from high school in the tenth grade! Although my formal education stopped there, I understand and know a bit more than your average tenth grader.

As I am writing this, I constantly change the music I am listening to, I get up and walk back and forth, I flip from one web site to another, talk to my wife, make some food and do many other things. It is not easy for me to stay focused on only writing this book. That, in a nutshell, is how many of us ADDers work and play. By reading what I have written, you are probably thinking that through school I daydreamed and didn't learn a thing. I did daydream, that's for sure, and I did a heck of a lot of it. While daydreaming, I still take in everything around me, and I mean everything. It's nauseating sometimes. I figured it out much later in life. When I went to take my GED weeks after I finished my last day of school, I didn't study or even really consider the test. I did not think I would pass. In fact, I thought I would fail miserably. When the letter came in the mail, I didn't immediately open it. I did not need another reason for my father to be disappointed in me. My mother is the one that finally opened it. After reading it, her face lit up and she informed me that I had passed. I can't tell you how relieved I was! I was happy I passed and now had a GED, but let me tell you quite honestly, I was more concerned about getting into more trouble and being punished than anything else. A few minutes later, after the initial celebrative mood wore off, I was indeed in trouble again. My mother was convinced I always had the smarts in school and that I was just too lazy; that I had passed the GED on the first try seemed to prove her theory.

My parents took me out of school because I was attending a Department of Defense school in Germany, and for American students who attended that were not affiliated with the military, their parents had to pay tuition. The tuition was expensive. My father had recently retired from the military and was starting his own business. He had already paid for a year and a semester of high school in which I did not receive passing grades and therefore decided that he could not afford to send me to school anymore. Consequently, when I passed the GED on the first try, my parents became enraged and were convinced I was just lazy and did not appreciate the financial burden I had put on them. Did I say it was tough being a kid with ADD? From that day forward my father put me to work at his business until I found a job elsewhere when I was eighteen. During those years, I was given very little free time and worked almost every day for twelve to sixteen hours. My father was not yet a forgiving man.

For the record, I never wanted to fail any class. My last day of high school was the most torturous day I have ever experienced. I have been severely punished and ridiculed in my life, but the last day of tenth grade will go down as my worst day ever. On the last day all my friends, classmates, and teachers saw me walking from class to class, collecting my grades. After leaving each class, they would see me pale, with tears welling up in my eyes, until my final class when I could not hold back my tears any longer. I was required to collect my grades from each of my classes and turn them in to the counselor on my way out since I would no longer be enrolled in high school. For other students this might not have been a big deal, but I was one of those unique students who didn't have a passing grade in any class. As I went to each class and handed my card to each teacher, I received a pitiful look and then the unforgiving mark next to the name of that particular class. I felt as though everyone I passed in the halls knew what was on the card and that I was being removed from school because I was a terrible, horrible student. I felt low. I had never experienced so much humiliation in my life. Just writing about this experience takes me back to that day and the emotions I felt. I feel cold, humiliated, and ashamed and I want to shut the memory away from my life. Twenty-one years have passed since that day of excruciating pain. I don't think the memory of that day, and all that it involves, will ever fade away.

How I passed the GED confused me probably as much as it confused my parents. Honestly, I didn't know any better at the time. It was many years later that I finally understood how and why. What I have come to learn is that people with ADD/HD take in every little detail around them, and it becomes impossible for them to concentrate on any one thing. We start daydreaming as a way to shut out the overwhelming amount of information coming at us, but in reality, we still receive all of the information. That is how I passed the GED and explains why I did so well on many tests and quizzes in school that I had not studied for at all. To get passing grades in school there are so many other variables than simply excellent grades on tests. It wasn't enough to pass classes in school, but it was more than enough for me to pass the GED.

Another very important factor is that the ADD/HD mind processes information in a different manner than a non-ADD/HD mind and I am not exactly sure how it works. I can read a book today and not be able to remember most of it when I am done. Another person with typical comprehension skills can read the book and answer questions accurately directly after reading it. The ADD/HD mind takes in information from the book as they are reading and processes each word and situation subconsciously and seemingly, for no reason, months after reading a book I will completely understand it in more detail than the person who could answer all questions directly after reading. Schools are not set up for the way I process information, and their curriculum can often be a nightmare for an ADDer.

It is very difficult for ADD/HD students to do well in a normal school environment. Schools follow strict guidelines and timelines, and have a standard curriculum for all students. Without proper psychological help, medication and coaching, an ADD/HD student has a very difficult time dealing with the typical structure of school and is more likely to tune out. Education in a structured environment is not always ideal for everyone, and it did not work for me. My mind went in any direction it wanted. Whenever I became interested in a certain subject I would become hyper focused in it, ignoring all of my other classes. The hyper focus that we ADDers are famous for would kick in and I would seek out all the information concerning whatever it was. I would study things in all ways possible, never satisfied with one point of view or one conclusion. For example, if I became interested in computers, I would not only study how to use the computer, but I would also study why the computer is useful, why various people use a computer, how to sell a computer, what the market share of certain PC companies is, and more. At one point in my career, I became a manager of the computer and electronics departments for my company's overseas division. The departments for these specific categories are the largest in Europe and in the company I work for. Within the first four months as manager, I increased sales in computers by nearly eighty percent and continued to increase sales in my departments every quarter after that. For my accomplishments, I received the second highest award in the company. I wrote a paper, "Building the Business", for the company concerning the computer and electronics departments, suggesting how we could build more sales. Many of the suggestions I offered in the paper eventually became corporate realities.

Because ADDers are extremely creative and need high stimulation, we tend to create things that will stimulate our own minds. The creations we come up with not only tend to capture our attention, but have the added benefit of capturing other people's attention. Think about that for a moment. If it takes something very stimulating for us, how would that same intense stimulation affect someone who is normally stimulated by less? This is the reason why the inventions and work of ADD/HD people are so sought after and successful. The artwork of Leonardo da Vinci and Michelangelo are well known and widely appreciated, and they were both great artists. However, Leonardo da Vinci's artwork is not only awe-inspiring, but it is captivating beyond comparison. He also created many innovative engineering designs, and drew beautifully detailed studies of the human anatomy. Leonardo is famous for keeping copious journal notes in which the handwriting is in reverse and can only be read easily with a mirror. What is most interesting to me is that Leonardo is the one who is believed to have had ADD. Learning that Leonardo da Vinci is thought to have had ADD, I can really understand why his work is still considered more distinguished than even Michelangelo's. Typical of ADDers, Da Vinci finished very few projects and was often in trouble for not completing commissions. But, what is even more typical of ADDers, is that Da Vinci had a very creative mind, which was never really appreciated to its full potential during his time. He also wrote extremely insightful scientific interpretations, which are considered to be ahead of his time. His designs and ideas are respected today more than they were during his lifetime. ADDers are extremely intuitive, creative, and often have unconventional ideas so that sometimes it takes a while for people to realize how amazing their creations and ideas really are. Being considered as ahead of his or her time is a frequent characteristic of ADDers.

Reading books is good for anyone, and it was especially helpful to me. A particular set of books was especially beneficial. Two series of books I enjoyed are by David Eddings, *The Belgariad,* and *The Malloreon.* His writing style is straightforward, and most of the good characters in the novels follow basic rules and make common sense decisions. Eddings also makes it clear what the bad characters are doing wrong, and how their decisions affect everyone. Both *The Belgariad* and *The Malloreon* are stories about a young man on his journey into manhood, the changes he must face, and decisions he must make. I read these books multiple times during my breaks and off time while working in my father's business. I often fell asleep reading them. These stories are complex and take place in a very detail oriented world with various races and many different personalities. Extremely intriguing to me was the economy David Eddings created and one particular character named Silk. I learned a lot about the real world's economy through the eyes and actions of Silk. Silk is an assassin and thief, but also a prince and shrewd businessman. Another book I read with many characters with common sense taking great risks was *The Stand* by Stephen King. It's not what I would call a horror novel, but it does have its scary moments and deals with good vs. evil.

I do not think anyone will find these books as standard reading in school or even consider them as educational. Still, I found them easy to read and understand and they had many good examples of characters making good use of common sense. I also read *Spider-Man* comic books growing up. Spider-Man is a character with many moral decisions to make who goes through some hard times. Without his costume his character is a regular person with regular problems, who has to find solutions to those problems. Spider-Man's alter ego, Peter Parker, seems very real the way he deals with ordinary, everyday problems. I enjoyed reading *Spider-Man* as a kid, because it gave me a better understanding of morals, using common sense, and that the decisions we make can affect us.

Authors David Eddings, Steven King, and many other writers create captivating stories with complex worlds, economies, diverse cultures, and their own histories. They also develop sensible characters which face realistic moral situations. They describe in splendid detail what these characters do, what decisions they make, and what motivates them. They effectively illustrate the positive characters use of good common sense. I found the common sense aspects of

Eddings' fiction very realistic and easily applicable to the decisions we make in our everyday lives. I think Eddings novels are very educational and should be a standard part of every school's curriculum.

7

Broken

Reading about different characters and their personal struggles helped me better understand myself and the world around me. Many characters use common sense and their own wit to help them in difficult situations and to survive. I was trying to get through my childhood by finding ways to deal with the negative criticism and punishments I received from my teachers and father. Growing up with undiagnosed Attention Deficit Disorder was not easy. I grew up feeling as if I was a bad person, dumb, lazy and that I couldn't do anything right. At times, I felt like an outcast or a mutant such as the ones in the *X-Men* comic books. We ADDers have very amazing abilities when we learn to work them and control them, but our minds do not conform to the normal thinking patterns. Whatever the name or idea, we are different in that we think differently. Our minds work and process information differently and that can be frustrating for a parent or teacher to raise or teach an ADD child – most especially if the ADD is undiagnosed. Often before ADDers are diagnosed, the ADD child grows up thinking that he or she is just bad or dumb, and feels like an outcast. We are also extremely intuitive and can sense what people are feeling and what they mean by just observing them. ADDers are also keen observers of human nature. I tried to survive my intense existence, not only learning about myself, but also observing people and learning what motivates them.

I remember as a very young child I was flamboyant and extremely energetic. Yes, I had many hyperactive and impulsive traits, but I learned very young to pay attention to my elders and act accordingly. I had to read every situation in an attempt to stay out of trouble and avoid punishment. My energy went into maintaining awareness and keeping quiet, still, out of sight. Funny thing is my father later complained that I was quiet and never talked to him or anyone else. Yes, I was very quiet when he was around. Even friends of my parents and teachers always commended me on how quiet and well I behaved I was. I was a very good boy in that respect and if I wasn't, I would feel the wrath of my father. I was a survivor, as I guess many other ADDers are.

Unfortunately, for me, being quiet and still was not the complete answer to staying out of trouble. I was terrible in school and no matter how hard I tried, there was no avoiding the consequences. One day when I was in the sixth grade, I came home and my father was waiting for me at the dining room table. He wasn't happy. A teacher had called him and expressed concern about my education and apparent lack of interest. Instead of trying to find out what was causing my problems in school, my father used his anger to try to make me conform and do better. Without explaining to me what exactly the teacher had discussed with him and without any effort to try understand me, my father told me to go to my room and bring him my bowling trophies. A few years earlier, I had started bowling on a team on Saturday mornings. At first, I wasn't very good, but it was fun and I had some talent for the game. My teammates gave me encouragement and were always positive, and the coach took time with me and taught me many nifty tricks of the game. Bowling gave me a sense of accomplishment and a feeling that I could fit in with others. Over the few years that I bowled, I became rather good at it and was fortunate to be on a very good team. We won three first place team awards and many other trophies. I put those trophies on my bedroom dresser and took great care of them. Admiring those trophies always gave me the feeling I could do something and be someone special. At that time in my life, I was not feeling very confident about myself in anything else.

Therefore, that day when my father told me to get them, I walked slowly to my room, with tears welling up in my eyes. I knew what was going to happen and I knew I was powerless to stop it. As I walked into the hall leading to my room, I spotted my older sister, in the doorway of the bedroom she shared with my little sister. My older sister and I usually fought like cats and dogs, but at that moment, she looked at me with sympathy and compassion. Suddenly I understood that I was in bigger trouble than I could hope to yet understand. I went into my room and just stood there for a few moments, my body already starting to shake. I just stared at my trophies. I allowed myself to stare at them, all together, being proud of them and of myself for winning them. Suddenly I heard my father yell out my name with a fierce voice, and I quickly grabbed two of the trophies, the lesser valued ones. I valued all of my trophies of course, but I had hoped he didn't want to destroy all of them, so I took a couple third place ones. I set the trophies down on the table in front of my father. He told me to be a man and to stop crying as tears were rolling freely down my cheeks. He took the two trophies and banged them hard against the floor. Pieces went flying everywhere. I had expected it to happen, but the shock of the experience rocked my body.

I was so afraid of my father, I could not say a word. I could only watch in horror. He ordered me to go get all of them. He stood up and his fists were curled. I ran back to my room, swooped all of the trophies into my arms, carried them back to the table, and set them in front of him. I set them down carefully, afraid to let even one drop. I had to be very careful not to provoke him. I was trembling uncontrollably and even that worried me, but I couldn't stop it. He stared at me with rage in his eyes and asked me why I was so bad, why I couldn't be smarter, and why I couldn't listen – so many "whys" and I had no answer. I whispered that I didn't know. That was the point of no return; he smashed all my trophies, one by one, onto the floor, and into a million shards of plastic, marble and tin. At that moment, I felt as though he had destroyed my accomplishments and my world. I was devastated. He asked me if making him mad was what I wanted, and if I wanted to embarrass him and my mom. My mother wasn't home and she couldn't save me this time. My father was furious with me that day, and he wanted to hammer his point into my mind for good.

I had hoped that the trophies would be the only targets of his rage. I was fearfully awaiting the spanking that was sure to come next. Instead, he told me to go back to my room and bring him all of my comic books. Oh no, I thought! My comic books were what I used to pass the hours and I read them repeatedly. I prized my comics so much that I kept each one in the best of condition, only flipping through the pages as delicately as possible. My father knew what I held dearest and he meant to destroy all of it. No words could describe the sorrow I felt. Unexpectedly, my older sister snuck up behind me while I was in my room. I never thought my older sister cared about me; I thought she hated me. I turned around and she was there. She looked at me but didn't say a word. She grabbed a large handful of my comics, ran silently back up the hall, and disappeared into her room with them. She had never done anything so nice for me before this and I didn't really know what to make of it. I was grateful though. I don't know if she ever knew just how much what she did had meant to me. I was starting to fall apart emotionally, but knowing she had saved a small portion of my comic book collection helped give me the strength to survive that day.

After I had brought hundreds of my comics to my father, who was supposed to love and support me, proceeded to rip each one of them in half in front of me. I began to tremble so violently that he finally looked at me with some concern and sent me to my room. He told me I was on restriction for the week and that I could not eat with them that night. I went back to my room and closed the door behind me. In the past, I would have curled up on my bed and cried myself to sleep. That time I didn't even make it to my bed and I don't think I shed a single tear. I fell to my knees on the hard wood floor, and just sat there for hours holding my arms around my shoulders trying to calm my trembling, but it just seemed like it would never stop. I was always in trouble for something. I had to be so careful, so very careful and consider everything I did. I didn't want to make my dad mad again, but I would, and I knew I would. I just didn't feel like I had the intelligence that other kids seemed to have. I felt stupid and worthless, and I felt like the best thing for me was to run away or die. Sometime later that day, my mother had come home and I could hear her through the walls yelling at my father. She had a temper herself and they fought for hours. I think she had threatened to leave him. I don't really know, because the walls muffled the actual words and I was still sitting on the floor in my room trying to stop from trembling. Later on, she came to my room, and I didn't know if she was mad at me too, so I backed away a little bit. She lifted me up gently by the shoulders and helped me to the bed. She didn't say a word; she just stroked my hair back and held me close, and then I started to cry uncontrollably. I never felt so helpless and it was such a relief that my mother still cared about me.

My father had been mad at me before, but that day, when he destroyed my most prized possessions, it was more painful than any punishments I had ever received from him before. I felt emotionally broken that day in my room, and I don't know if even today I am over it. Before that day, I was a somewhat happy go lucky kid, and had some confidence in myself. Okay, I knew I was not good in school and punishment for that was always a real possibility and that I still had to be cautious. However, after that day, my father made me feel so low and so worthless that I no longer had any foundation to stand on. I became even quieter and more careful of my actions. I stayed further and further away from my father, trying to avoid him at all costs and barely spoke to him when he was around. It not only affected me around him, but I became withdrawn around others too. I found myself constantly flinching when anyone made sudden movements or seemed angry with me. I did what I could to survive and the best tactic for me was to keep to myself and be as quiet as possible. I was even determined to do better in school, but my schoolwork became worse and worse. After an ordeal like that, who could have expected any other outcome?

I remember a day in seventh grade when I was called to the counselor's office. The counselor wanted to talk to me about my schoolwork and my lack of interest in all things concerning school. I just sat quietly. He asked me several questions as to why this and why that. My only answer was either silence or my famous "I don't know." Eventually the counselor informed me that he was going to schedule an appointment with my parents. When he told me that, I completely panicked. I didn't even think of my actions or remember to be careful. I started to beg and plead with him not to call my parents. I was trembling and exasperated. I could see the surprise and fear on the counselors face. I had been sitting there perfectly composed for the longest time, and then suddenly I was screaming, begging, pleading, and trembling. He tried to calm me down and when he got out of his chair I shut up and stared at the ground, but I did not stop trembling right away. Somebody had come in behind me, and the counselor got up and left the room for a few minutes. When he came back, he said I could go and that's the last time I ever talked to that counselor again. He must have realized that I was distressed. I don't know if he ever contacted my parents, but I don't think he did. If he had, I am very sure I would have found out the hard way.

8

Father's Influence

Reading about my experiences with my father might make you believe he was a mean person. I agreed with that thought for a very long time. I do not have any children, but with maturity and what I have learned about ADD, I think I have come to understand the frustrations he must have felt trying to raise a son who had undiagnosed Attention Deficit Disorder. I do consider his form of discipline harsh. However, after finally being diagnosed with ADD, I can see why he may have been at his wits end with my behavior as a child as well as some of the conflicts he might have experienced.

ADD can be and often is hereditary. It is possible that I inherited ADD from my father. He seemed to have many ADD traits himself. When I was growing up, he was always lost in his own thoughts, impulsive, hyper focused on his particular interests, and he was attracted to highly stimulating activities and people. He was also very easily frustrated and often in search of the quick answer. With ADD, there is no quick answer. Learning to live with ADD and recognize when it is affecting my life is a day-to-day task. I have been doing many things habitually for most of my life and changing that, which requires focus and structure, is hard work for an ADDer. Knowing that having ADD is not my fault does help me overcome some of the problems caused by it. Knowledge is the key to a better, more fulfilling life for any ADD sufferer. When I finally understood that I had ADD and what it is, I felt as if a huge weight was lifted off my shoulders. I beat myself up for who I was and what I was doing for a very long time. It was such a relief to find out that I was not simply lazy and there was a reason why I could not conform to rules and be like everyone else.

ADD children need encouragement and personalized attention, and most importantly, they need positive, constructive feedback. A young ADDer must already deal with the fact he or she does not function like other children. An ADDer child often looks, walks, and talks just like any other typical child and yet they seem to stand out as an underachiever. There is nothing an ADDer child wants more than to do well and achieve. Really, when it comes to our interests, hobbies and talents, we are overachievers! When we constantly fail in a structured environment, we are not only punished, but we think less of ourselves. Nobody can punish an ADD child more than the ADDer child can do to him or herself. It is impossible to correctly treat the symptoms of ADD or any illness without a proper diagnosis, and if it is assumed that there is nothing wrong, that makes the suffering much worse. Denial can be detrimental to a child's development. One of my major lifetime habits is to repeat myself. This might not be a direct ADD symptom, but I usually repeat myself due to the severe discipline I received for my actions as a child. I was often fearful and spoke softly, almost not wanting to be heard. As a result, I would frequently have to repeat myself. A child who is undiagnosed and is an unrealized ADD sufferer must contend with constant reprimands, and eventually develops habits to cope. Some of those habits make the child appear afflicted with other ailments. Depression and suicidal thinking is common in a person who has grown up with undiagnosed ADD. Having low self-esteem and depression in addition to having ADD, is a recipe for a disastrous life. Therefore, on purpose, I repeat myself. Denial can be detrimental!

How much blame can I put on my father? I don't really know, and I don't know if putting blame on him for anything will help me at all. He may have been as frustrating to his parents as a child and received the same harsh punishments he gave me, or worse. The way he treated me was perhaps the only way he knew. After all, the old-school mentality was to discipline a child for doing things he or she was not supposed to do or for not following instructions. Using a belt or putting a child to work was commonly used in order to make a child obey. It was somewhat beyond consideration that a child could not obey due to an unobvious disorder. If a child looks perfectly healthy in appearance, what could be the problem? When there was a problem, the solution was to bend him over one knee and correct his wicked ways! It was done that way when I was growing up. My father was raised that way and he tried to raise me that way. He grew up to become successful and to raise a family, so why would he not think that wouldn't work with me? Considering that it wasn't working with me must have caused him even more anxiety and anxiousness, causing him to be even harsher. Should I excuse him then? Let's consider a bit more information first, before I answer that question.

For a very long time I thought my father's anger towards me was my own fault. I have since learned that it is common for children to blame themselves for the way they are treated. Children make mistakes, and being accountable for those mistakes is a part of growing up. Their behavior should be corrected to help teach them to become responsible adults. Unfortunately, my father chose to correct my mistakes using violence or verbal abuse, which had a dramatic, negative effect on my self-esteem and my sense of security as a child. There is no excuse for abuse or severe physical punishment. A child may have some understanding of his or her actions, but not to the same degree of understanding and compassion an adult should have as a grownup raising a child. A child should feel empowered by his parents; a child should feel safe with his parents. Adults who have decided to have and raise a child must accept all the responsibilities that are implied in such an important decision. A child cannot help being born normal, with a handicap, or with ADD. It is not a choice. Parents should try to find an understanding for their child's behavior that may include seeking medical advice. There are parents who refuse to admit, or fail to recognize, that their child may have a problem, and therefore could jeopardize the child's emotional and social development. No matter how hard a child is slapped, beaten, or scolded he or she will not improve. Punishment will not cure a child of any health problem or behavioral disorder.

Some parents just do not realize that their child has a learning problem, and are simply confused by the issues presented. Sometimes these parents love their child so much that they give into the belief that their child is just not smart. They do not punish them; instead, they resign themselves to believe that he or she will probably never be successful. If a child is having problems in school, that may or may not indicate he or she has ADD, but it certainly does not hurt to seek a professional analysis. It may reveal something easily treatable. By all means, never give up on a child. By removing me from school, I felt my parents had given up on me and I blamed myself. It was a terrible, lonely feeling to have. Although I forgive my father for his actions, I do not completely excuse him. There is simply no excuse for severely punishing a child.

Often, I wish I could have spent more quality time with my father, just him and me doing regular father and son activities together with no criticism and no work. He was usually so busy though. I remember having a genuine good time with just him and me one time in my life. One day when I was playing in the backyard, my father came outside to see me. I was nervous about why he wanted to see me since I was afraid of him. He asked me if I would like to take a walk. As a child I never disagreed with my father or told him no, but I didn't know what to make of the situation. He wanted to take a walk with me in the woods. We had a wonderland of forest area behind our home. I had spent a lot of time exploring those woods when I could, and knew the paths well. As we walked, my father was just casually talking to me about different things. He asked me what I liked, and what kind of games I played. Our conversation was simple and pleasant; we did not discuss anything serious or threatening. We walked for about a half hour when we came upon a lush green area in the middle of the trees. It was a vacant camping site. Strangely enough, a softball and bat were in the clearing, so my dad picked them up. Although it was a beautiful, sunny day, the ball and bat were wet. The wooden bat looked like it had been outside for a long time, but that didn't matter. My father started to pitch the ball slowly towards me, and I tried to hit it with that old bat. We did that for hours until the sun started to set and we had to leave. Before we left, he told me to hide the ball and bat underneath some brush behind some trees so we could find them easily whenever we came back to play. His words excited me, so I hid the ball and bat very well, and made a mental map of the area. I know that if I were to go looking for that bat and ball today, they might not be there, but I certainly would find the hiding place. Sadly, we never returned to play together again. We had such a grand time – I remember it fondly. It was one of the only times my father spent so much quality time with me. He had it in him to be a great person and a decent father. It was one of the most wonderful days of my life growing up. I don't know if my mother put him up to it or if he did it on his own. That moment I shared with my father, on that beautiful day, is one that I treasure. It enables me to forgive my father for the way he disciplined me for my inexplicable behavior as a child.

A few days after our day together in the woods, my dad took me out and bought me a terrific new bike. The bike I would eventually lose at Phil's house. I had told him that I wanted a bike and he remembered! Our relationship seemed to be improving. A change seemed to be on the horizon. The disassembled bike was still in the box in our basement for about a week after he bought it. He wanted to put it together for me, but he was so busy that he never found the time. I asked a neighbor if he would put it together for me and he did. I was so happy. My mother saw me riding the bike and called me over to her. She asked me who put the bike together and I told her. She said I should have waited, and that my father had been planning to put it together for me. My shoulders slumped with the realization of what I had done. Even today, I can feel the remorse I felt upon hearing my mother's words. He never said a word about the bike and yet I think that I hurt his feelings. I felt that I ruined, and thus lost, any real chance of developing a closer relationship with him. The opportunity to bond with my father meant a lot to me, and yet I lost it like so many other things in my life.

There is another aspect to be considered in my relationship with my father. He did not try to foster a good relationship with anyone that I can remember. He did not spend too much time with my sisters either. He took us places on family vacations, but he always seemed distant and disinterested in us. When I was about eight or nine, he would often take me to a lake to go fishing. But he never really fished with me. I usually fished alone, while he went into the clubhouse to play cards. He was a man who was standoffish, kept to himself, and never really seemed to have any close friends or someone with whom he hung out consistently. Every now and then he would seem to get along with someone, and then soon I wouldn't see that person again. When I consider how he was socially, now that I have a better understanding of the characteristics of a person with ADD, I can somewhat relate to him. Developing and maintaining good relationships for someone with ADD can be a struggle because we have a difficult time recognizing verbal and non-verbal communication cues from others. ADDers can ramble on when they talk and can get off track during a conversation. Moreover, we tend to interrupt others while they're talking, and not listen to what is being said. Breaking plans or commitments with others also makes it difficult for ADDers to do well socially.

I've never been good at staying in touch with friends. There are times when I hang out with them a lot and then other times when I seemingly forget about them. Many people at work consider me a "thinking" man because I am always quiet and appear deep in thought. The same could be said about my father. He was a thinker. He was always contemplating and didn't want to be disturbed. When he was like this he didn't have time for others. I do not remember my father ever mentioning old friends he might have had. I don't really think he kept in touch with anyone from his childhood. There is nobody I keep in touch with from childhood except on occasion when they contact me.

I do not intentionally ignore friends. It's just that sometimes I simply have too much going on in my mind to think of them. I can go weeks or months, sometimes years, without thinking of people who are important in my life. Those people are still important to me. I miss them and I don't miss them. It is very difficult to explain. My mind is always occupied with multiple thoughts and considerations. It does not slow down enough to consider the consequences of neglecting my friends. It is not easy to be my friend and it is not easy for me to maintain friendships. My best friends have always been people who do not require a lot from me. These friends are usually undemanding, positive towards me, and do not criticize my mistakes. I have been criticized for as long as I can remember and I don't want to spend my time with overly judgmental people. I have friends who reinforce me positively. The friends I have know I make mistakes, but they do not vocalize or criticize them. They like me for my positive qualities, and hang out with me for fun and camaraderie. Over time, the friends who last are the ones who get to know me and like me for who I am. They know that I am not always going to contact them, but somehow they understand that I want to be their friend, and therefore they choose to contact me. When friends contact me, it takes me out of my thoughts and sort of awakens me to their existence again. Almost as if I have short-term, selective amnesia. When they make contact, I suddenly remember the friendship fondly, and want to go out and have some fun with them!

I don't know the reasons why my father didn't have any close friends or why he was always in a thinking mode.

When I consider that I am my father's son, I see that we are alike in many ways. I may have inherited some of the ways I am and the ADD from him. I believe he wanted a successful son and had very high aspirations for me just as he had for himself. I also think he may have had ADD and he did not *feel* successful. He ruined many opportunities for himself and our family due to his own risky behavior. His frustrations were put in plain view with me, a son, whose behavior he probably recognized all too well. He may not have wanted me to follow his example, so he disciplined me harshly for every mistake I made. He wanted a son who was an excellent student, who could become a doctor or a lawyer; not a son who could barely sustain a D average in school.

When I finally had my own job and was out of the house, my father always asked how it was going and if I was a manager yet. At eighteen, I had no interest in becoming a manager of anything; I was more interested in just surviving on my own. I did not ask him for any help. I found my own apartment, my own car, and my own job. He had nothing to do with any of it and I was proud of that. When I came home to visit, I barely spoke to him, though I talked to my mother all the time. Once I was out of the house and out of my father's control, my mother became more important to me. I realized she was happy for me and a bit relieved that I was out of the house. She wanted to help me in any way she could. She still thought I was lazy, but the most important thing for her is that I was taking care of myself. I could call her or come by to see her anytime. I liked that she would cook something for me on a moment's notice, if I ever wanted something to eat.

I suppose in my own way I punished my father for the way he punished me as a child. My personal reckoning with him was not deliberate but I think it was far more effective than anything I could have planned or wanted to do. I ignored him and whenever he asked me a question, I would answer with either a yes or no and give nothing more. I could tell it frustrated him. I didn't care. I didn't want to hear anything about what I *should* be doing or how I *could* be doing something better. He always wanted to give me helpful advice, which usually included him reminding me that I was an underachiever, lazy, and would never amount to anything anyway. Ironically, his predictable disdain and disapproval of me eventually motivated me to become more successful. It served as a catalyst, which got me to start using my hyper focus, my creativity, and my common sense more to find ways of becoming a success. It made me hunger to accomplish something. I am a believer in the law of attraction, and that hunger within me started attracting me to opportunities for success. I understand now that I wanted to become successful despite my father, and that I was determined to prove to him that he had nothing to do with my success. In reality, he had a lot to do with it, but not in the way he probably intended. I realize now the influence he had on my becoming a success. He probably never knew just how significantly he affected me.

9

Inspiration

Ever since I was a very young man, I always felt I was destined to do something great, even through the hardships I endured. I have never been able to put my finger on exactly what it is that I would do, but it has always seemed to be just over the horizon or around the corner. The feeling I had is similar to searching for a word that is on the tip of my tongue, but it still escapes me. I did not want be average nor do something mediocre; I had a desire to be great at something. That desire put a lot of pressure on me, which drove me to discover that I could be outstanding at billiards. They say when the student is ready the teacher will appear and something like that happened for me.

I started playing pool when I was about nineteen. Phil, who was very good at it himself, introduced me to the game. I was also good, and a natural at it. I loved the game, not only because I was good at it, but also because it allowed me an escape. I could go to the pool hall and play for hours, just hitting the balls around, allowing my mind to drift off wherever it wanted to go. It is a wonderful feeling to do something you enjoy and at the same time just relax and not worry about too much. At least that's how it started out. Because I was rather good at playing pool, people started to take notice of me. I started to receive compliments on my game, and others wanted to play with me. I became so popular that I had to start coming to the pool hall when it wasn't busy just so I could get some time in for myself. The more I hung out at the hall, the more people started putting thoughts into my head about playing for money and participating in tournaments. In the beginning I didn't know too much about the world of pool, so I started reading some magazines and watching it on television. Suddenly, I wanted to be better than anyone else and I wanted to become a pro and win tournaments. Since I had not been successful in school, and I had a rather low self-esteem. Playing pool well raised my confidence. I began to think that I would do something great in my life, and that I could *be* someone; a champion pool player.

Within a year of starting to play pool, I entered some tournaments and I had some moderate success. The more I played in the tournaments, the more I was noticed, and within just a few short years my name was fairly well known throughout Germany for my excellent pool playing. This was great for me! I loved the recognition as much as I loved playing the game. As successful as I was becoming, I knew I had a long way to go. After a few years of playing, I wasn't really advancing anymore. My performance was inconsistent in tournaments. I would do very well for a match or two and then I could not make a ball to save my life. I was having problems. I didn't know it then, but I was having typical ADD problems. Sometimes I could not stay focused on my game because I became too distracted by the activity going on around me. Trying to tune out the distractions was difficult and so frustrating. It drove me crazy and plagued me to different degrees throughout all the years that I played. I realized that I needed to make some changes in my approach to my game and was able to improve slowly. The first step I took toward improving began with some insight from a very unlikely source. I guess this student was ready and the master appeared in the form of a wonderful young girl.

In 1992 I met Dennis, who has a sister named Jennifer. He became a very good friend with whom I'm still in contact with to this day, even though he now lives on the other side of the world. His sister was attending school in the U.S. at the time, and I did not meet her right away. Dennis and I hung out almost every day because he was intriguing and exciting to me. We would go out racing cars and goofing off all the time. Some of my best experiences were just having fun with him. He didn't really require much from me and I didn't really require much of him. He liked to come out and watch me play pool, and occasionally he placed side bets on my games. He loved the excitement of the halls, and enjoyed watching pool played at a high level. He played pool too, but he didn't pretend to be more than a recreational player. He could have been really good if he wanted to be, but he enjoyed watching the game more.

That next year at Christmastime his sister, Jennifer, came to visit him. I was invited to his house the first weekend she arrived. He was eager for me to meet her. I fell for her the moment I saw her. As I entered his family's living room, she was sitting there on the sofa appearing beautiful and magnificent to me. She was prettier than I could have ever imagined. She was a slim, seventeen year old girl with long, straight, red hair which was parted just enough to show her delightful face, and she was wearing glasses. I could tell right away that she was most likely extremely witty and intelligent, and probably much smarter than I was.

When we met for the first time, Jennifer smiled and looked at me somewhat funny, almost as if she already knew me. Perhaps that was just my wishful thinking! Her voice was pleasantly sweet. We connected immediately that day. Later in the evening, by the time everyone else went to bed, we stayed up and talked like old friends for hours, until the sun rose the next morning. Our conversation was easy and natural; it wasn't awkward or strained and neither of us were nervous. She told me about her life growing up, and I told her a bit about mine. She stayed in Germany for three weeks and we spent nearly every day together.

Jennifer seemed extremely mature and insightful for her age. I was very impressed with her. She graduated high school at sixteen and was already in college studying pre-med. We talked about everything, including life's challenges, and of not knowing what is in store for us in the future. She happened to be at a crossroads in her life then and was not sure who she was or what she really wanted to be. She mentioned that she felt she was destined for something special but that she did not know what it was. She explained how the feeling and the knowledge was at the edge of her consciousness and she just couldn't reach it yet. She talked about the same feelings I had experienced when I was younger. When she spoke of this, I felt a moment of rapture because I could relate to her on a deeply personal level. I was thrilled to discover that we had similar concerns, hopes, and desires. Due to the many challenges of my upbringing, I had kept this thought in the back of my mind. I never talked to anyone before about my feelings of becoming something great. Finally, talking to her about it gave me a sense of validity and purpose that I desperately needed. She had much to say about it and I could tell it was very important to her, perhaps the most important thing in her life. She told me that she felt lost and was doing things that were expected of her, but not necessarily what she wanted to do. Surprisingly, she was an insecure person even with her incredible intellect and accomplishments. She was mainly insecure because she could not figure out what she was supposed to do with her life. She said that she couldn't talk to anyone about this, and that I was the first person she mentioned it to in such detail.

Our conversations were always splendid and insightful. We allowed each other to speak freely, finish whatever it was we were saying, and then we offered feedback to each other. Our moments together were surreal and equally beneficial to both of us. Finally, I decided to tell her of my desires to become someone extraordinary, to do something great that would benefit others, and to be someone I could be happy being. It was the first time I had ever talked to anyone about this, and when I started to talk to her, I became very emotional. She listened intently and compassionately to me as I opened up to her about my deepest feelings. She helped me realize that my true desire was to be an accomplished individual and to be loved unconditionally. Because of all my years of being a failure and being ridiculed, all I wanted was to be a success, have others be pleased with me, and to be happy with myself. She even went on to explain that in order for others to feel good about me, I must first feel good about myself. And that in the end, it would be irrelevant what others thought of me as long as I felt good about myself. She told me that she could tell I was a very good person at heart, someone who cares about others and yet doesn't know how to show it, or is unwilling to show it for fear of being seen as weak.

My conversations with Jennifer helped me begin to find myself. I still wasn't too sure how I was going to achieve what I wanted in life, but I felt I was on the right path. I had managed to break free and live on my own, start my own life, and I was making a name for myself. The things I wanted and needed were coming to me because I was attracting them to me whether I fully realized it or not.

Jennifer came into and out of my life just like that. We spent three weeks together just talking. I think we helped each other in ways neither of us would fully realize for a long time. I have met many people in my life, some I have known for a long time and some for a very short time, but rarely do I remember conversations with any of them with such detail and clarity as I remember my conversations with Jennifer. When it came time for her to return to college, we meant to stay in touch, but didn't. Neither one of us was ready for a relationship of such meaning. We had a lot to learn about life and ourselves on our own. Regardless of the incredible connection we had, I felt it was our destiny to have been there for each other at that moment and then go our separate ways. I think we understood what we meant to each other for those three short weeks, never denying any of its special meaning.

Indeed, meeting Jennifer was a life changing experience. She was the master who appeared when this student was ready. She came into my life at a time when I needed guidance and was open to it. I have learned that if we want something enough, the universe will move to give it to us, and Jennifer was exactly what I wanted and needed at that time in my life. Playing pool was the most important thing to me at that time. I talked to her about my ambitions and troubles with the game, and she helped me realize that my life's ambitions and troubles were mirrored in what I enjoyed most. She pointed out that in pool I was learning through trial and error, and that my experiences in school were limiting my progress. I had failed so miserably in school and held such a disdain for criticism that I would not allow anyone to give me lessons. She told me that not all lessons are filled with criticism and that many people have trouble learning in school and still do great in a one on one environment, which is tailored for them. She also said that I was highly interested and motivated to learn and to become a better player. I never had such motivation or desire in school. I was also very protective of my accomplishments and did not want to share them. I felt if someone gave me lessons, that somehow they would take the credit for my wins. I listened to her advice and eventually improved my game exponentially. I felt my desires for greatness becoming a reality for the first time after I met Jennifer.

10

Recognizing Talent

A few weeks after Jennifer returned to school in the
United States, I beat a professional pool player for the
very first time in a tournament. He was a great player and I
beat him rather handedly. I was humble with the win on the
outside, but on the inside, I was bursting with excitement. I
had achieved something I truly wanted and was distracted by
it the rest of the tournament. I lost the next two matches, and
was eliminated from the tournament. It shocked the
professional who had lost so quickly to me. That was okay
for me. I was calm and knew that this would be a one-step-
at-a-time journey. I was so overwhelmed with winning that
one match, I became hyper focused on it and was distracted
the rest of the tournament.

I was usually very boisterous when I did well. I was
my own marketing machine who made myself bigger than
life to others, making sure everyone knew when I won and

whom I had beaten. This put more pressure on me and I was discovering that pressure helped me focus.

To be jovial and boisterous about accomplishments is very common in many ADDers. And unfortunately, we feel extremely depressed when we fail. I understand this well because I have experienced these emotional extremes quite frequently. However, I learned to control these emotional extremes to an extent by being more aware of what it is that I am doing. Understanding that we are reacting too intensely to things without justification helps us lessen the emotional strain we put on ourselves. Sometimes we simply have to remind ourselves that the world is still under our feet and tomorrow brings another day. I used to walk around with the weight of the world on my shoulders, believing that everything I did was ultra important. Believing that helped me focus, and at the same time was emotionally destructive. Without the proper diagnosis of ADD, many of us find ways to improve our focus and concentration on our own, which are not always the healthiest for us.

I wanted to improve my game more than anything, and slowly I began to do just that. After I came down from the high of winning against the professional player, I traveled with my friends to observe a major tournament in Munich. It was the first time I saw what a professional tournament was like. The highest caliber players from all over the world attended and we had perfect seats. I was more than impressed with the ability of the players. I was in awe. I had never seen such performances before and it gave me a glimpse of how pool was meant to be played. There were so many styles and so many personalities. My mind absorbed everything around me like a sponge, and by the time the tournament was over, I was instantly a better player.

Although I didn't know what it was called at the time, I was experiencing osmosis at that tournament. Today, I consider osmosis to be the number one advantage of my ADD and I credit it for much of my education, especially in school. For instance, osmosis enabled me to pass the GED. I understand osmosis to be an ability to learn through forms of observation and to absorb information on a less than conscious level. Osmosis gives me a unique ability to learn and understand nearly everything I encounter, sometimes quickly and sometimes over time. I can influence how quickly I learn through osmosis by my interest level and by the amount of pressure I put on myself to learn. The more I hyper focus on something, the more I absorb it. At times I felt as though I had hidden powers; strengths beyond my imagination. The extreme pressure my father put on me to do well in school when I was a child was not constructive. It was a destructive kind of pressure, which lowered my self-esteem.

Observing that professional tournament in Munich put me in the right mindset to take the next step toward improving my game. It was the perfect primer. I discovered what I wanted to learn, and I had a better idea of what I wanted to become as a player. Things just seemed to be coming together for me. As fate would have it, a few weeks after that tournament I continued traveling with my friends to a few pool halls around the country, and one of the halls we came to was owned by that same professional player I had beaten weeks earlier. When we arrived, he was playing a money match with another player who was not a pro but was considered the better player. We watched for several hours. While we watched, I was informed that the owner's opponent was an American service member named Chance. He was a cool player with an even cooler name. I liked him immediately.

That evening I took the opportunity to meet Chance and played a few rounds of pool with him. Word got around that I had beaten the hall owner in a tournament recently and, as a result, Chance invited me to play with him in a doubles match as his partner. I played okay that night, but not nearly as well as I could have. After the match, I decided to take Jennifer's advice and ask Chance for lessons. He said he would consider training me because he was looking for a doubles partner. This was more than I expected. He also placed a steep fee on lessons. It would cost me to learn from him. The fee was a bit higher than I could really afford, but I agreed to it. I suddenly had several reasons to pay attention and the pressure to learn was an advantage for me.

I learned a lot from Chance. I advanced in my game more than ever before. He not only instructed me in the mechanics of the game, but also the mental game behind it. It turned out that the mental aspect of pool was even more vital to my growth as a pool player and a person than the mechanics. Moreover, I made another significant discovery concerning mental pressure. For most people mental pressure causes them stress, frustration, nervousness, and loss of concentration. For me, though, experiencing mental pressure was increasingly becoming an advantage, which helped me to focus on my game better than ever before. Sure, my mind would still drift occasionally while I was playing, but the risks involved in losing a match kept me aware of it. I learned to refocus my attention back on the game where it belonged, rather quickly. I taught myself to hyper focus at will. Learning to control my ability to hyper focus was a major breakthrough to improving my game. So major, in fact, that I was becoming a serious contender in the world of pool in Germany. In Kaiserslautern, where I live, house tournaments were held once a week in the local pool halls. I had participated in them off and on for a while, not really doing that well. There were some great players in Kaiserslautern and competition was fierce. I never really considered myself any better than the other players in the community. However, there came a point after I learned to focus that I won 22 out of 25 local tournaments. Winning so many tournaments was no easy feat for any pool player on any level, but for me this was an amazing accomplishment with so many obstacles to overcome. I was at my best in the final matches when my hyper focus really kicked in under the extreme pressure. I rarely made mistakes that late into a tournament, and I could see how the pressure was negatively affecting my opponents. Although I didn't know what ADD was yet, I discovered how to control one of the advantages of ADD while playing pool. Previously, I considered my ability to hyper focus as a disadvantage because I didn't know how to control it. I still had problems controlling it in other areas of my life, unfortunately.

Winning so many pool tournaments made me such an attraction in the local pool halls that I started receiving a lot more attention from the people there. I admit that I enjoyed and appreciated the attention, but somehow I started to doubt myself again. This type of pressure, the pressure to perform at the expectations of others, was new to me and I wasn't prepared for it. I started to lose at pool again and to lose my confidence. My confidence increased with my recent success at pool, but was not strong enough yet. I reverted to doing what I was good at, which was to fail, to embarrass myself, and to feel hopeless. It is really no surprise considering I had lived nearly my whole life with a self-defeating negative attitude and a depressingly distrustful belief in my abilities. As I lost more and more matches, thoughts of the past crept back into the forefront of my mind. I remembered my brief episodes of doing well in school, when I would become ecstatic, followed by my depressing fall back into the oblivion of failure. I didn't have the type of support an ADDer needed when I was a child. For so long in my life I felt as though I was incapable of doing most normal things. That somehow I was cursed and that it was my destiny to repeatedly fail. I don't know how many times I laid awake at night wondering why things had to be so very difficult for me. Many times I fell asleep with tears in my eyes, wondering why I even bothered to try. Most of my life was one long endless pity party. I thought that it was just my reality and that I should accept it. Those thoughts of dread and self-loathing continued to haunt me until I changed my way of thinking. The wonderful thing about us ADDers is that we are resilient fighters, and we are not quitters. No matter how hard I tried to just give up and accept my supposed fate, my inner desire to be successful and to do something special would not allow me to simply hang my hat and call it quits. It was at this time that I met someone new, who helped me change my way of thinking and who would propel me even further down the road of success. When I changed my way of thinking, I began to see the positive results of thinking about and doing things in a new way.

Every pool hall has its regulars, and not necessarily players, but people who enjoy watching the game or those who like to invest in talent. Pool halls are places of action, places where shooters come to duel, where money passes hands, and pride is always on auction. Pool halls, in some places, can be very dangerous, and if you're going to play, you better be serious and have the cash. In some places it is better not to play, even if you have the cash. A person could end up in trouble quickly. I never weighed any of the dangers. I enjoyed the tension and the risks involved. It seemed to add a little missing flavor to my life. Besides, I didn't consider anything in our modest town to be risky, but then again, ADDers hardly ever do. ADDers are notoriously known for being impulsive and taking unnecessary risks, as if we have no ability to sense danger. We do not always weigh risks in the same way as others might. We want to be stimulated, and being impulsive and taking risks provides the stimulation we crave and need. Even so, it is important to learn balance and recognize danger before it is too late. I had a keen awareness for danger and yet I frequently put myself in situations that could be considered dangerous.

There was a fellow American who frequents the pool halls I played at, whose name is John. He is an older gentleman and a successful, private business owner. He is well off and he liked to bet a lot of money on me to win. At first I didn't really know who he was. I usually ignored people I didn't know. I didn't ignore them simply to be arrogant or stuck up. As you have read, I was not very good at making conversation, especially with people I didn't know. That has changed, but back then I just didn't try to get to know people. I stayed close to myself and didn't let too many people in my space.

I suppose it was obvious to him that I was having some sort of problem since I was losing more frequently than I was winning. John walked over to me and decided he would have a talk with me. Not too many people approached me on a personal level then. I was closed off and was known not to get involved in idle conversation. My attitude towards people I didn't know did not deter him though. He is a person who has seen a lot and knows a lot. He sat down at my table as I watched my opponent deliver another loss to me. He did not talk for a while; he just sat there. When I started a new match, he informed me that he was betting half a grand on me. I just stared at him. At first I felt like calling him a fool. I didn't. Everyone knows John and everyone is well aware that John is no fool and very protective of his money. He told me that if I won he would give me half the winnings. Now he had my full attention. I played better, but I didn't win. John continued to sit there. He bet again as I started my next match. I wondered what the heck he was thinking. At this point, I started to tune out everyone in the pool hall. I was feeling a new kind of pressure, one that could result in a valuable reward. I won the next match and then the next. I didn't lose anymore that night, to anyone.

When the place closed down for the night, John handed me a fist full of cash and said he would see me here the next night. He didn't ask me, he simply told me that he would see me. He had caught my attention and he knew it.

I showed up at the pool hall the next night at my usual time. A few minutes later John arrived. I sat at the bar alone, waiting and becoming edgy. I never liked waiting anywhere for anyone. Even for short periods, waiting makes me feel fidgety and testy. I had to wait a bit longer as John made his way through the pool hall greeting several people as he went. He knew many people and they all seemed to like him. John was always smiling and in a good mood. He finally came over to me and asked me how I was doing. I asked him if he had a game lined up. He didn't. He told me that he liked me, liked my game, and that I was a fine pool player. I became frustrated with him and told him that I knew I was good. He kind of laughed and ordered a drink. He told me he had something for me. He took something out of his jacket pocket and handed it to me. It was a blue paperback book, which had obviously been read quite a bit. It was tattered and the title was broken apart by deep creases. I read the title aloud. It was *The Power of Positive Thinking* by Norman Vincent Peale. I looked at John as if he was insane. He told me to read it. He wanted to develop a business partnership with me, which involved playing pool and making money.

I agreed to the partnership, and over the years we made a lot of money. John and I became more than friends. I consider him a valuable mentor, and when we meet, he never cares if we have a match to bet on or not. He is someone who likes action, but even more, he is someone with a lot of heart and has the ability to see when someone could use some help. He helped me find my way again when I needed it. For as long as I have known him, he has been helping people with his caring attitude and his sage advice.

The Power of Positive Thinking is an inspiring and thought provoking book I recommend to anyone. Positive thinking is one of the most powerful mental strengths a person can have. The book describes how having an enthusiasm for life, work, or anything, in combination with positive thinking, can enable us to free our minds of the mental obstacles that we have put in our own way, which normally inhibit us from living more fulfilling lives. Once I started reading it, I could not stop turning the pages. I started to see clearly how my negative thinking was affecting me every day in so many ways. I can't say that I changed and became a positive thinker overnight, but reading it helped me begin to change the way I thought about situations and myself more positively. I started to use positive thinking daily and I began to feel more confident in myself. I began to recognize that when I thought positive thoughts in connection with my desires, those desires would usually become reality for me. The hard times came when I succumbed to my old ways of negative thinking. It took a while to change my thinking and I did need help. I did not know I had ADD, but I realized that I wasn't leading a productive, happy life as others were, and that I felt depressed more frequently than I felt happy. I finally went to a therapist for help, and it was one of the best decisions I ever made. Through therapy, I learned to think more positively about my life. Positive thinking changed my fundamental thought process in a revolutionary way, and helped me become successful in many areas of my life. Choosing to think more positively has helped me feel better about myself, achieve more professionally, and overcome many negative aspects of having ADD.

As ADDers, especially those of us who are undiagnosed, it seems that there are so many things against us. We often have to deal with and conform to the structure of the educational system, social structures, and expectations from others and ourselves. There is so much negativity attached to having Attention Deficit Disorder that often we are compelled to keep it a secret once we are diagnosed with it. If so much is against us, why in the world do we add ourselves to the list? Thinking negatively or being ashamed of having ADD is counterproductive to living successfully with it. As ADDers, we already face the challenges of making our way in a world which is not set up for our unique way of processing it. If we want to become successful and happy, we should encourage ourselves to think more positively about ADD and ourselves. Positive thinking changed the way I viewed the world around me, and thus the way I responded to it and interacted with it. Once I started thinking positively, I began to see new possibilities for myself that I had been oblivious to before.

Another thing that is positive for ADDers is to develop their natural talents and pursue their interests. We are very talented people and developing those talents can be beneficial to us in many ways. I am a talented pool player and by playing and improving my game, I learned as much about myself as I did about pool. Before I started playing pool, I associated with as few people as possible. Today I am both a business manager and public affairs representative for a global company. Pool taught me how to focus, plan, and become more sociable. ADDers may not be born with such structure skills, but we can learn them. It is difficult for an ADDer not to be interested in something at which they naturally excel, and they can learn to develop that talent in a way that works for them.

In pool, a ball can be missed by just being a millimeter off course. Each shot must be thought out with the consideration of the following shot. Many of the top players map out each shot of the game before they even take their first shot. To go from one shot to the other, certain planning must be considered. Pool players must also adjust to factors away from the table itself. We must consider whom we are playing against, and the styles presented must be registered, considered, and overcome. We must also learn to control all distractions, which are deliberately caused by our opponent. It's not always a fair game and this applies to all players, not only ADDers. Pool requires intense mental alertness, and therefore mental conditioning is a constant in the life of a pool player. The mental conditioning I learned and achieved while playing pool has helped me in all other areas of my life. I have been able to take control and direct my own mind. This is amazing for someone with ADD. It goes to prove that even if you have ADD, you can learn to control your mind and change the thoughts which randomly surface. To condition one's mind for the positive and train it to work in a manner that is desired requires a lot of effort, energy, tenacity, and emotion. I often found myself wanting to give up and, frankly, on occasion I did give up. Still, my strong desire to exercise my talents, no matter how difficult it became to advance and no matter how many times I gave up, always led me back to the table to keep trying.

Recognizing and developing our innate talents can give us the power to overcome many of the negative aspects of ADD. By pursuing and engaging in my talents, I was determined to find ways to develop the skills needed in order to take full advantage of them. I believe that even if your talent is not something which will support you financially, it is still important to develop it. Some ADDers find financial success using their talents. I am a good example of someone who engaged in a specific talent and yet was not able to support myself financially with that talent. I always held a day job, but by fostering my talent in pool, I discovered that I had many other abilities. One unexpected talent I developed was the ability to charm a crowd. As a pool player who often attracted crowds, I became a sort of showman. I didn't do this intentionally; it happened over the years as I became more and more comfortable with people watching me. I eventually found it easy to make crowds laugh or amaze them with some kind of antic. I could talk to the crowds and interact with the people with ease. Being social was a serious problem for me. There was a time when I was very uncomfortable being watched and it caused me to lose a lot of games and at times it kept me home, away from what I loved to do. That's how powerful pursuing one's talents can be.

11

Double Life

W hen I turned twenty-seven I realized that I was rather lonely for personal companionship. I had not met anyone until now that I felt I could settle down with. I figured that at my age, settling down and getting married was expected and would help me become more like everyone else. I met a nice girl named Carmen around this time who was everything I was not. She was organized, efficient, and nice to a fault. Her life was very structured. I liked her a lot, and felt being with her was the right decision. She helped me associate better with my coworkers, and she tried to help me in many other ways. When I talked to her about work and the things I was doing there, she pointed out many things that I was doing wrong. I realized, essentially, the biggest thing I was doing wrong was just being myself.

When I met Carmen, I had been working for several years at a mundane job as a receiving specialist in a warehouse. My job was very simple; it entailed checking in packages and their contents, and then processing that information into a computer. There was nothing complex about my job; it required following a few simple steps to accomplish the same task everyday. I worked Monday through Friday, from seven o'clock in the morning until four o'clock in the afternoon. I rarely even had to think in this particular job. However, it was the perfect job for being a pool player and having a social life. With my evenings and weekends free, I could practice and play pool to my heart's content and spend time with my friends. My job, though, drove me bananas and made me physically sick. Enjoying a social life outside of work and having time to play pool was great, but it was also at a great cost. I spent forty hours a week in a job that wasn't suitable for me. Having ADD and working in a very mundane environment day after day wrecked my nervous system. The worst part of it was that I worked with people who were perfectly content to sit and do their lackluster jobs all day. They were nice people, but I didn't understand them and as a result, did not get along with them very well. I was always clowning around in order to spice up my tedious workdays, which got me in plenty of trouble. I was lucky that I was never fired from that job.

I felt as though I was living two lives. At night and on weekends I was a sort of celebrity pool player where my antics were accepted and even praised. During the day I worked in a routine job, which bored me beyond reason. The people I associated with at night were wired for action, whereas the people I associated with during the day were focused on accomplishing tasks in a standard, efficient manner. Sadly, this contrast was most noticeable to me when

I would return to work after a big tournament or pool event. I remember playing in the world championships of Russian Pyramid Billiards. It was taking place in Germany and the main sponsor of the tournament invited me to try out. I always had a great time and I loved such events because not only was it great competition, but also many of my pool-playing friends, who I related to well, were there. After a weekend competing and socializing with very talented, famous, and interesting people, it was anguishing for me to return to work. Whenever I went to pool tournaments, I was well received and the people there seemed excited to see and talk to me. I was appreciated for my talent, manner, and my personality, even though I didn't always win the tournament. I dreaded returning to work where no one knew who I really was or what I could do. I kept that other part of my life to myself because I didn't really think the people at work would care if they did know. Playing in pool tournaments and working at a dull job was an emotional rollercoaster ride for me.

After a while, I got to a point where I resented my day job. I didn't think I could find a better job because of my education. I simply couldn't quit, because it afforded me a paycheck that allowed me to live my life as a pool player. And if I did find a better job, I may not be able to continue playing pool full time. I was faced with a dilemma, or at least I thought I was. I knew there wasn't much money to be made playing pool anymore. Germany was experiencing an economic recession at this time and, as a result, many big-money tournaments were being cancelled. Realizing that I could not easily make a living playing pool, I began to consider seriously making a major change in my life.

Being with Carmen helped me improve at work because she was very supportive of me and firmly believed that having my day job was the right thing to do. When I would mention my aspirations of playing pool full time as a professional, she became worried that I would quit my job and pursue something that was less financially secure. With Carmen I began attending work- related social gatherings. Everyone from work liked her; she blended in well and got along with just about everyone. Getting along with everyone was not something I was good at and finally, thanks to her, I was at least socializing with my co-workers and superiors. My situation at work was improving, and I did not realistically see myself doing something different. Carmen and I were also getting along quite well at this time, and we decided to get married.

Once Carmen and I married, she became more critical of my behaviors. She complained that I was not very organized nor did I keep track of things well. Therefore, she took care of the bills, when she could find them. I put letters and bills in piles and rarely sorted through them, which caused me to pay late fees more often than not. This really frustrated Carmen. She said that I embarrassed her, especially when we were around her family, when I became completely engrossed in something interesting, to the point of ignoring everyone around me. If I was reading a book while we were at her parents´ house and her father tried to talk to me, sometimes I would not hear him or acknowledge that he was talking to me. This is one example of many where I apparently disrespected her family. Carmen would get so angry with me. My ADD had not yet been diagnosed and it seemed to her that I was doing things on purpose, much like my parents had thought. It really irritated her when I would become bored and decide to go for a long drive. She would inevitably call me on my cell phone and berate me for missing lunch or dinner with her parents. Once, I got lost while driving around her parents' city alone. When she called, I told her I was lost, and instead of helping me find my way back to her house, she scolded me over the phone as if I were her naughty child. Being treated like that was a poignant reminder of my childhood, and it was the beginning of my slow journey away from her.

One interesting thing was that I did really well when her older sister and her family visited us or we visited them. Her sister and husband had two wonderful children, with whom I got along well. I joked and played around with them all the time and this pleased Carmen. The hardest part about our divorce later on was that I would not see those kids again. I seemed to relate to kids well, because they could do what most adults could not do, which was keep my attention.

My own sisters have children now too, and I have a very special relationship with them. I like being around them and they enjoy being around me. We entertain each other. In many ways, I am a big kid at heart and I relate easily to the energy and excitement of children. My sisters loved it when I entertained their children and they could do their own thing. I was the preferred babysitter and very protective. I think kids deserve consideration and attention. I suppose I tried to treat my nieces and nephews as I wanted to be treated as a kid. I spoiled the heck out of them too. My sisters and Carmen didn't appreciate it when I overindulged my nieces and nephews, but I did it anyway. Children deserve to be spoiled every now and then. It was painful for me when my sisters eventually moved to the United States. I miss them and I try to stay in touch to let them know how much I am thinking of them every day. I am terrible at staying in touch with anyone. My sisters don't understand how hard it is for me, and they frequently let me know how I have neglected their children. When I think about contacting them, despite the convenience of email and telephones, most of the time I either put it off or forget about it. Often I considered moving back to the U.S. to live closer to them, but regrettably my own self-doubt and the security of my albeit dull job kept me from doing it.

I tried hard to change for Carmen and eventually decided to stop playing pool as often and give my day job my full attention. It turned out to be the wrong thing to do for myself. She did not make me stop playing pool per se, but she wanted a house and more security, and I wanted to make her happy. Therefore, I tried. Over time, she became increasingly disappointed with my ways and me. We started to drift apart as I began to realize the things she wanted and needed were not things that I cared about much. For a while, I felt so chastised by her that I started to feel as if I was back in school. It came to a point where we did not talk to each other very much anymore and she'd get so mad that I would stay away from home. After work I would go play pool first for several hours so that by the time I got home at night she would be too tired to argue.

It was during this time that I went to a doctor for treatment to help me figure out why I persistently felt so bad physically and mentally. I was usually sick to my stomach, had constant headaches, and felt emotionally exhausted. My doctor recommended psychological therapy to help me resolve my issues. I began going to therapy regularly and it help me more clearly understand myself and also what was affecting me so strongly to make me physically sick. Therapy helped me realize that I put a lot of pressure on myself to be someone that I was not in order too please someone else. Slowly, the more my therapist helped me learn about myself, my motivations, and my behaviors, I started to feel better physically and mentally. Through therapy it became more obvious to me that Carmen and I were not in sync as a couple and that perhaps it was better we were not together. I was reluctant to leave her because she is a nice person on many levels and she helped me become a better person in many ways. However, we were becoming more and more disconnected and that only increased her anger in the way I was. There came a point when we completely stopped talking for a while, and when we started talking again I told her that I did not think we should stay together. It was the first time I had brought this up and she fell apart. I felt so bad. I decided to simply drop the subject and continue to try because I didn't want to hurt her. Carmen was very emotionally fragile, and that was the most difficult thing for me to deal with. I wasn't well equipped to deal with her sometimes, and I did what I could to console her during her emotional ordeals. I was not very good at it. I considered myself a neglectful and bad husband. I had failed at nearly everything else, so this was not such a big surprise to me. Carmen and I would stay together for another two years. She never argued with me again after I suggested we separate, but our relationship was strained after that. Our life together was tearing both of us apart. We did not understand each other and my tendencies still upset her. Her choice to remain quiet about it only caused her to become more disenchanted and depressed. We were wrong for each other and it was more hurtful to stay together.

I grew up with the dream of marrying once and staying together forever. I am a very romantic person and had the vision of that perfect marriage. I had even wanted children and hoped one day that would become a reality. In my relationship with Carmen, things were so difficult and emotional that we decided children would not be a good idea. I no longer thought I could be a good father. I was far too neglectful.

In other ways, my relationship with Carmen motivated me in a direction to be better. I had enrolled in my company's upward mobility program. Since I decided to stop playing pool full time, I had more time on my hands and I was determined to try to please my wife and make my marriage work. I continued going to therapy, but was not diagnosed with having ADD yet. ADD is a disorder, which was not and still is not well known or understood by German doctors. My doctor, Dr. Gary, believed that my problems, physical illness, depression, and low self-esteem were the result of my upbringing. He helped lead me down a road of self-discovery, whereby he helped me recognize many of the positive traits and skills I did have. He clearly pointed out to me how I already used them in my life to survive. At first, he believed I specifically developed these skills to survive. Later, when we discussed the possibility of me having ADD, we discovered that the basic symptoms I had been dealing with all my life and the skills I used to counter these symptoms were all indicative of having ADD. It took years before a diagnosis of ADD was confirmed because Dr. Gary originally did not believe ADD to be my case. The delay was not only because ADD was not a well-understood disorder in Germany, but also because I originally sought help for the depression and the physical ailments I was suffering from, such as the headaches. Dr. Gary's goal was to help me relieve the depression I was experiencing. I had been depressed for many years for many reasons, but mainly for the way I was. We worked through most of my issues of self-doubt and depression, and I learned ways to focus on my strengths more. My therapy helped me lift the fog of my depression and to improve in several areas of my life. However, that was not enough; it became apparent that something else was affecting my thought process and my behaviors.

Therapy gave me a better understanding of myself and my abilities, and gave me a feeling of confidence at work. I became a better employee and was doing more at work than simply receiving. I completed my work faster and looked for additional things to do. Around this time was when I began to multitask. ADDers are fantastic at doing multiple tasks at the same time. It is because ADDers are very rarely satisfied with the mundane. We like excitement, risks, and we like to keep our minds busy, going from one thing to the next. When we take into consideration fidgetiness, impulsiveness, and overall lack of patience, all of these traits are compelling reasons why we are so great at multitasking. At work, I have often found myself with a boring assignment unable to complete it, but if I have several assignments, I am able to complete all of them easily. This wasn't always the case, but today it is thanks to years of mental conditioning as a pool player. Pool players are always multitasking and always considering several different scenarios at the same time. When applying what I learned at the pool table at work, I found that I was able to complete much more when I worked on many tasks at one time. Multitasking helps me be more efficient at work, and it allows me to inject excitement into my predictable workdays. The ability to multitask is one of my ADD traits that work for me.

It took a long time, but I learned many ways to use my innate abilities for my own benefit. I did not know I had ADD and yet, in order to survive, I had no choice but to find alternative ways to do things. I think this is true for all ADDers. We learn to compensate for the way we are if we want to succeed in a structured world. This also helps explain why many people believe we ADDers grow out of our disorder. When we start learning to live with our unique ways, people tend to think we are functioning normally as responsible adults, and not the distracted, daydreaming children we once were.

With Dr. Gary's help, I noticed that I completed more tasks when I didn't try to concentrate on just one thing. I found ways to change things up. I also started to stay at work longer, mainly to give Carmen time to relax at home. She was usually her most sensitive when she came home from work, and I found it was better to give her quiet time to herself. My improvements at work were not going unnoticed and before long, I was promoted into a better position. It had been years since I had done any formal schooling and this time around, in the upward mobility program, I found myself doing well. The program was not completely similar to formal schooling as it was a more interactive experience, and I found most of the information and lessons to be fairly common sense. I completed the program at the top of my class and afterwards was offered a management position.

As I started to excel at work, gain more self confidence, and discover more about myself under Dr. Gary's care, it became ever clearer to me that I was in a relationship that wasn't right for me. When I asked Dr. Gary to help me stay with Carmen, he asked me to think about what I wanted from the relationship. I gave it a lot of thought and the only answer I could come up with was that I did not want to stay with her. This tormented me because she is a decent person and didn't deserve to have someone give up on her. At the same time, I knew that I would never be able to make her as happy. She needed someone who was more organized, consistent, and had clear goals. I was not ready to be all that for her and I felt caged. The worst part of it for me was that I felt parented by Carmen. The last thing in the world I wanted was to be parented by anyone and that caused me to be rebellious. I distanced myself more and more from her. I stayed at work longer, absorbing myself in learning my job. I knew that she sensed I was distancing myself from her, and for her own reasons she did things to try to bring me closer and save our marriage. She wanted a house for us, so she hired an architect and began actively looking for land on which we could build. I did not join her in her search, but she was determined to secure our relationship and future. I was not yet ready to admit to myself that the relationship would not last and did not dissuade her from looking. Nonetheless, our relationship did not last and we divorced less than a year later.

12

Time to Forgive

As the time to leave Carmen drew closer, memories of my father weighed on me because one of the last things I ever told him was that I was getting married. My father died shortly before Carmen and I got married. He died knowing that I would marry and I believed it pleased him in some way. I didn't hate my father and when he passed away, I loved him deeply despite our difficult relationship. My father was a planter and loved flowers. After he died, Carmen took some of the plants and flowers from his house and replanted them in pots at our home. I never talked to her much about my father, and she did not know how he had treated me as a child. I appreciated her sentiment, and never had the heart to tell her that I would have preferred those plants and flowers not be a part of our life. Although I had forgiven my father, I still did not want to be constantly surrounded by reminders of him. Learning that I have ADD has helped me resolve the issues I had with my father growing up, and helped me release the resentment in my heart for my father.

I tried to punish him when I got older and moved out on my own. When I think about how I treated him then, I feel that I may have punished him more severely than I ever realized before. I had completely ignored him after I turned eighteen. When he tried to talk to me, I ignored him as if he wasn't in the room. He never mentioned or reacted to my indifference, he just said what he wanted to say at me whenever I happen to be around him. I never responded to him or answered his questions. I did not plan to ignore him or make a conscientious decision to treat him with disdain. It just happened, as if it came naturally. I did not enjoy it when he talked to me and tried to give me advice. I did not want him to be any part of the decisions I made for my future and myself. I had no desire to discuss anything with him because he always had a painful way of sharing his negative opinion of me and telling me the way I should be living my life. He did want me to be successful, but the ways he suggested I go about it, such as going to college or joining the military, were not reasonable for me. It was as though he did not know me and forgot how miserably I failed at school. He never seemed to care how or why I performed so poorly at school. But he did show me in no uncertain terms that he cared when I did badly at school. He used severe punishment to show me that he cared about my education and development. The brutal discipline he chose for me when I was a child seemed to be his answer for me as an adult. He suggested I join the military. He thought that perhaps the order and discipline of military training would be good for me and change me. I did not know I had ADD, but I knew there was no way in the world I could survive the military's regulated lifestyle. I was doing well enough to keep myself on track with the things I wanted to achieve. The military is a fine career for many people, but I believe that for someone like me, it could be catastrophe. A person with ADD cannot be forced to conform, act, or think like everyone else in a structured environment. Changing a person's behavior who has ADD is not that simple. That is why my father's punishments never worked with me. I was sure that if I joined the military, I would be kicked out for my behavior and inability to follow strict guidelines. I didn't need to be diagnosed with ADD to know how I was as a person. The mere suggestion of joining the military, and what he implied with the suggestion, infuriated me. I accomplished a great deal playing pool and I never shared that with him. He never got to see me play, and I never invited him to watch me play until he was dying. He did not see any of the trophies I won. I did not purposely keep him from watching me play or hide my success from him. I disconnected myself from him and did not share anything with him concerning my life at that time. I was living and succeeding at pool on my own, and I didn't want him to think he had anything to do with that. Sometimes he would offer me some good advice and, only because it was from him, I would ignore it and do something completely different so that it would seem as though I did not take his advice seriously. ADDers can be extremely defiant and I am no exception.

I am no longer angry or resent my father for the way he treated me. I know that can't change the past, so I try to put it behind me and move forward positively with my life. It never really dawned on me that I loved my father until he started getting sick. My father was a big, tall, strong man, who reminded me of a tough John Wayne character. When he started to get sick, a softer side of him started to show through. It wasn't just that he was more vulnerable now that he was ill, it became clear to me that he was sad too. He always hid any sentimental emotions he had behind his facade of toughness. The sicker he became, the more depressed he seemed. I understood that he was in a great deal of physical pain. I think he was sad because he knew that he had a terminal illness, and that he would not be able to fully realize the plans, aspirations, or the reconciliations he had wanted for himself. I began to see my father in a different light when he was ill, and realized how short life was for us.

For ten years before he got sick I treated my father with contempt as a way to show him I was mad without ever telling him directly that I was mad at him. I know now that I did not do it consciously, but as a reaction to how he treated me as a child. Sadly, I think he received the message loud and clear. Punishing my father the way I did to get back at him seemed like the right thing to do when I was eighteen. I was compelled to settle the score with him then. He hurt me, and I wanted to hurt him back. The way I felt about my father changed as I got older, achieved my own success, and gained more self-confidence. When he became sick, I realized that he did not deserve to be punished for doing the best he could as my father. I wanted to reconcile with him before his death. I don't know if we both found closure, but I would like to think that we did. With cancer spread throughout his body, my father was continuously in extreme pain. He could barely leave the house and often he was delirious. For the first time in my life, I tried to connect with him. I knew he wanted to be a part of my life and I knew, even if he did not say it, he regretted many things he did. He was bed ridden, so I would come over to the house and watch pool videos with him. Although he was not able to watch them very well, I would talk to him about them while he laid there in his bed. I talked to him about things that were going on in my life. I did not know that his death was imminent and tried to give him hope by inviting him to come see me play pool. It was very important for me to connect with my father and to let him know that I loved him. In those final days of my father's life, I felt very remorseful and wished I could have been a better son. I thought of all the things I could have done to build a good relationship with my father. We did not have a real father and son relationship and I truly felt it was my fault. Not knowing I had ADD, I blamed myself for being the way I was, and truly believed my father deserved a better son.

Because I was often at my parents´ house during that time, I talked to my mother more frequently. She told me things that I did not know about my father. She explained to me that he was very proud of me, and that he did indeed regret many things which he had done. She told me that he was a different man before he went to Vietnam. He had come back distressed, and he angered easily. I realized that my mother had done a lot to protect me, and had threatened to leave my father if he did not stop physically punishing me. She had a difficult time too. She had a husband who was disturbed from going to war, and a son who just did not fit in or seem to try hard enough. She wanted to do things differently with me, but my father would not allow it. He was raised in an old school manner which dictated that a son's disobedience be solved with hard, swift discipline. Apparently it worked on him growing up, so he had every reason to believe it would work on me. I already knew that my mother cared about me deeply from how she changed after I moved out at eighteen. She was always there for me. She provided for me when times were difficult and was always there when times were good. I can certainly say that there were times I might not have made it on my own if my mother had not assisted me. She still seemed to believe I was lazy and often lectured me on how I could do better with my life. She did not lecture me out of anger, but rather as a concerned parent who wanted the best for her child. I still receive those lectures to this day and I have heard her give them to my sisters too. I know it's just her way of showing she cares and letting us know what her concerns are. Ultimately though, she is always there for us.

The last day I ever saw my father alive was one of the two days with him that I will treasure forever. He was in the hospital awaiting emergency transport to a specialized cancer treatment hospital in Texas. He was given morphine for the excruciating pain of his cancer, and therefore he was lucid and he wasn't feeling the pain. It was a very sad day because we knew there was not a lot of hope that treatment would be successful. Even if treatment went well, it would only have extended his life for a short time. My father was in relatively good spirits, perhaps due to the morphine. He was allowed to walk around the hospital and he wanted to walk to the cafeteria for something to eat. He asked me to walk with him. He seemed strong and robust again as we walked. He talked about things to do around the house, and asked me to do a few things for my mom while he was away. He was very concerned about the placement of their washing machine. He wanted to make sure it was placed exactly right so that my mother would have enough room to maneuver in the washroom. I had given him some billiard magazines to read when he was admitted to the hospital and he told me how his doctor was very interested in pool. He told me that he mentioned to the doctor that I was the best pool player. I was delighted when he told me this, and I could tell from his smile and the light in his eyes that he was proud of me. He was very pleasant and enjoyable to be around that day. He was suddenly being the father that I had always wanted. When we made it back to his room, he sat down at the edge of his bed and I can tell he had become tired. I knew I should leave and give him his rest, but I just didn't want to leave, so I lingered for a few minutes longer. When I finally put on my jacket to go, he said something I never expected. He said that he was satisfied with me. I was caught off guard by his comment and I didn't really know what to say. I simply said, "Thank you." A few minutes later, I told him that I loved him and said good-bye. Those were the last words I ever spoke to my father. He passed away a few weeks later on the night I arrived in Texas to see him. My sisters and I were all together when he passed.

13

Therapy

Writing this book is part of my cure for what ails me. Taking pen to paper, in addition to my therapy, has helped me flush out some of my most painful memories as well as help me remember some of the most pleasant ones. Good and bad memories go hand in hand. However, there are some bad memories that have a life of their own. They wake me up late at night from a restless sleep and have me pacing the floor for hours until dawn. After a while, it can be easy to forget the good memories. The best solution I have found is to discuss the most unsettling memories with my therapist and try learn what it is that is really upsetting me. This open dialogue with my doctor often helps me understand what is troubling me about particular memories. In some cases, I am then able to move on.

For a time Dr. Gary, my therapist, believed that I suffered from Post Traumatic Stress Disorder and that it was the primary reason for my problems. I can see why he felt this was the best diagnosis for me at the time. Some of my symptoms were similar to those in people who have PTSD. Sometimes I would experience strong reactions to situations in the present that triggered memories from a past traumatic event in my life, whereby I would feel as though I was reliving that painful experience from my past. For example, when I flinched at the sudden movements of my friend a few years ago, I understand now that I was actually reacting to the harsh punishment I received as a child. Unfortunately, I was also troubled by the painful memories I relived in my mind that weren't triggered by anything particular. Emotional triggers are not always required for me to relive the past. Being an ADDer and being such a daydreamer, I would often dwell on my memories, replaying them in my mind as if watching a movie. When Dr. Gary discussed PTSD with me, we did not yet know I had ADD. I wanted to take a moment and talk about the PSTD theory in my case because, over the years before I was diagnosed with ADD, I have been diagnosed with many other conditions to explain my ADD tendencies. This is not to say I do not have PSTD to a degree, however, ADD is the center of my issues.

The mind of an ADDer is extremely artistic and visual. I have the capability of visualizing memories in my mind with vivid clarity. With a mind that is capable of such detailed visual recollection, recalling painful memories can be extremely distressing for me. I often wondered why it was that when I slept, the most painful and negative memories would come to life. Dr. Gary helped me understand this by explaining that events which cause the most adrenaline to be produced are the easiest to remember. Adrenaline is a main ingredient to solidifying memories in the mind; the more adrenaline that is produced, the stronger the memory will be, and therefore the clearer it will be remembered. For ADDers who commit events to memory in great detail, their memories can cause a lot of pain long into the future. Dr. Gary asks me to talk about my most troubling and pervasive memories and then helps me understand why they may be upsetting. By exploring and talking about my most painful and recurrent memories with him, I begin to remember them more subtly and not so intensely. He helps me bring those memories to the surface and understand them with a fresh perspective and forgiveness. The forgiveness is not simply toward anyone who might have contributed to the memory, but primarily toward myself. Having undiagnosed ADD, I blamed myself for everything that happened to me because of the way I was as a child. Having a better understanding of my ADD now, and resolving painful memories by forgiving myself, has helped me find some inner peace.

Considering the vivid clarity of an ADDer's memory, I firmly believe that it is very important for parents and teachers to be aware that what they negatively say or do to a child, especially one with ADD, may be remembered with excruciating detail and possibly dwelled upon for years. Since we are creative in nature and react to stimuli intensely, it is quite possible that negative memories can build in our minds as we grow older, becoming stronger and perhaps more harsh. I do not write about my severest memories in the pages of this book. It really isn't worth it. Through therapy, and since I have been diagnosed, the impact of those memories has lessened. In this book, I write about certain memories which have affected me significantly but are not necessarily the most painful for me. ADDers like me are sensitive people who sometimes over analyze and regret their past decisions and actions. They usually feel that all that they do is wrong and are ashamed of their mistakes. My most troubling memories feel like they have a life of their own and play incessantly over and over in my mind. For me, it is difficult to move on, forget my mistakes, and put them behind me because I feel like I am continually repeating the same frustrating mistakes throughout my life.

As an ADDer, I am impulsive and often miss normal human communication cues. For example, when I am in a discussion with someone, I tend to over explain myself and not pay attention to what others are saying. I am allowed to present my side of an argument, and then I continue explaining in detail the validity of my argument at such length the other person begins to tune me out. What's worse is that I continue explaining even after that person has already agreed with me. Because I don't realize that they have already agreed with me, I end up talking them back out of their agreement. Regretfully, I don't always pay attention or keep track of what people are saying to me. We ADDers tend to do this with just about everyone and we always need the last word. The last word seems to be our reassurance that we were heard and understood. Often what we are really trying to do is avoid making a mistake, a repeat situation of something similar in the past. When we are asked to explain a situation, our mind goes into overdrive and we think of every possibility relating to that situation. We then feel compelled to vocalize all of it when we should be more concise. Later, after we have over explained ourselves, we relive the situation over and over in our mind, thinking about what we could have done differently, and promising ourselves that we will never do it again. It´s a struggle not to think about and relive these situations in my mind. Whenever I find myself in a similar situation of over explaining or being impulsive, I clearly recall how I behaved in the past, my body shivers and gets tense, and I feel frustrated and ashamed of myself. If such feelings would only last for a day or two it would not be so bad. These feelings can go on for days, during which I remember more of my blunders and then I berate myself up for not learning from past mistakes.

When I was eleven years old I had a good friend named Brian who I had only known for a few weeks before I met his sister Renee. Once I met Renee, my whole world stopped! It was a very dramatic moment in my life. I had never really taken notice of girls up until this point, but Brian's sister was the most beautiful creature I had ever seen. She had long, glistening brown hair and a walk of utter confidence. She was hip and I didn't even understand what hip was then. When I met her, she was out looking for Brian and thankfully, he was with me.

One day I walked Brian and his sister back to their house. When we got there, Brian was in trouble for something and Renee was fiery mad. It was amazing how her anger encouraged her beauty. I couldn´t take my eyes off her stunning features. After I left them, I walked back home unable to stop thinking of her. She captured my imagination and became my mind's one and only consideration. My hyper focus abilities were working overtime. I had never experienced such feelings before. Later that same evening, I went back over to Brian's house. Renee answered the door, and I was stunned to see her right away. Her beauty struck me again like a piercing arrow through my heart. She wasn't mad anymore as she was earlier in the day, and her features were relaxed and delicate. She almost seemed to be another person entirely. Her eyes had locked on mine and after a moment she said that she would get Brian for me. I told her that I actually wanted to talk to her, and asked her if she could step outside with me for a moment. She stared back at me with a puzzled look, and then stepped outside and closed the door behind her. Here was my moment and she stood there, just waiting. Without thinking it through clearly, I quickly asked her if she would be my girlfriend. Nothing changed in her facial expression, which was excruciatingly void of any hints at her reaction. She continued to look at me with that puzzled look. I figured she would tell me no, but to my surprise she didn't say no or yes. Instead, she told me that she would think about it. To tell you the truth, that was more than I expected. She was so beautiful and confident. I had expected her to turn me down.

I went over to her house every day after that and asked her if she had an answer yet. I did not know if she was just trying to play me out and watch me squirm or if she was really considering. Finally, after waiting for four days she gave me her answer on a Monday morning at school. That morning I approached her in the busy hallway at her locker and asked her if she had an answer yet. She said, "Yes." I was stunned, and I responded by saying, "Thank you!"

After I thanked her, I had no idea what else to do, so I walked away and made my way to my first class. Since then I have played that moment over in my mind, thinking of all things I could have done differently. I could have hugged her, kissed her, walked her to her class while holding her books, or just about anything other than walking away from her. How romantic! I beat myself up for that years later. She was my first girlfriend and I felt I ruined it from the first moment. I had no idea what it meant to be boyfriend and girlfriend or what they were expected to do together at that age. Perhaps I worried about that day far too much, focusing negatively on what was probably a natural reaction for an eleven-year old boy, and I should have gotten over it. I did not focus on the positive outcome of that day, that she decided to be my girlfriend and I got what I wanted.

For many years I thought endlessly about the time I spent with Renee. Remembering my relationship with Renee made me feel both wonderful and full of regret. We had so much fun together, but all I could think about for the longest time were about the things I had done wrong in the relationship. I thought about what I could have said to her or done for her. We were great together and our relationship lasted for about a year. Her dad got a new military assignment and they had to move away. I was devastated when she left, and for seventeen years after that, Renee held sway over my mind as the one I always wanted to be with. Yes, I had other girlfriends during that time and even got married, but I always considered Renee to be my ideal. My memory of her was always at the forefront of my mind, especially during hard times. I had a strong desire to find her and see her again. I finally located her online through a high school reunion site seventeen years after we had last seen each other. I was excited to finally write her and find out what she had been doing during the years that had passed. I wrote her and she wrote me back. We discovered that we were both married. She sent me her telephone number and I called her. Her voice sounded more mature, but it was still the same as I remembered it, and I was overjoyed to hear it again! I knew we would come in contact with one another again, somehow. She had been such an amazing force in my life. I enjoyed talking with her and finding out all about her and her life since I saw her last. While talking with her on the phone, I realized that we were very different people now. We did not have the same intense connection that I remembered when we were younger. We talked like long-lost friends and that's what we really were to each other. It was good to talk to her and it helped me a lot. Unexpectedly, finally making contact with her stopped me from hyper focusing on the memory of our relationship and her.

Thanks to my therapy sessions with Dr. Gary, I have been able to better understand and resolve past memories, as well as to remember more of the positive aspects of them.

The absolute best memory I have of Renee is when we walked home through the woods one afternoon, and we came upon a very large puddle, which encompassed our entire path. I think Renee tried to use the puddle to help me move forward in our relationship. We had been in our relationship for quite a while already, and although we were often together, I had never held her hand or acted like more than just a friend. Looking back, even at that age, Renee wanted something more from me, a sign of commitment, and the puddle was her opportunity to let me know that. At the puddle Renee was all giggles and smiles. She gave me a whimsical look and told me to carry her over the puddle. I did not expect that. My face went flush when she asked me, and I could feel my ears burning. She came very close to me, wrapped her arms around my neck, and told me to pick her up. This happened so fast, I could only do what she asked. It was better that way or I would have made a fool of myself. She jumped into the air and I caught her legs and held them next to my sides. She laughed, and to cover my nervousness I laughed with her. She weighed very little and I carried her over the puddle slowly. We were about 20 feet past the puddle when I realized we were already across it. She was in my arms and I didn't want to let her go. I let her down, slowly and gently, not really wanting to. It was the closest we had ever been to each other or ever would be. We laughed and goofed off all the way home. For a while, I thought our relationship couldn't be better than this, and then we started to drift apart.

In learning about ADD, I have come to understand why I did not recognize that she was trying to get closer to me. As I mentioned before, people communicate every day in ways that involved simple human cues to which people respond. People with ADD, especially kids, do not always recognize and notice these cues. Many ADDers like me are oblivious to subtle cues of communication between people. I think that is very important for others to understand and realize about us because it can easily be misconstrued. I am also convinced that this is a major reason that many people and doctors believe that children with ADD/HD grow out of it. It's not that we grow out of it, it is that we learn to better recognize what people mean when they are communicating verbally or non verbally. There came a time when I was growing up that I realized that I just didn't get what people meant when they communicated with me. In my teens I began to observe others more closely, read a lot books, watch T.V., and watch movies to try to learn how people communicate effectively with each other using subtle cues.

Looking back on my relationship with Renee, I know she must have been frustrated with me. I can remember many times when she tried to show me that she wanted to hold hands and be more personal. At the time, I had no idea what she wanted from me. Nothing she tried to explain, by her actions and subtle communication, came through to me. It must have been like talking to a hearing-impaired person without knowing sign language and not knowing the person is hearing impaired.

As it was with Renee, so it was with Phil as well. Phil was such a great friend of mine for several years when I was growing up, and I spent all of my free time with him. He was extremely popular and yet he considered me his best friend. I remember very clearly the day Phil stopped what he was doing and told me directly that he considered me his best friend. Because of my insecurity and my pessimistic nature, I failed him. He was certainly my best friend and yet I told him I had no best friend. He had done something which he was not known for doing and that was open up to me on a personal level, and I let him down. We never really clicked together after that day. If I had been strong enough and more aware of myself to tell him the truth, that he was indeed my best friend too, I do not think we would have grown apart. It is not a nice feeling to have hurt someone. Whether I wanted to or not, I hurt Phil, the only person who seemed to care about me and want to hang out with me during my painful early years of school. He didn't seem to care what others thought of me, and he knew that I had a lot of troubles at home and at school. Over the years that we hung out, we did everything together and were considered two peas in a pod by those who knew us. Even when Phil tried to set me up with girlfriends and I ruined those chances, he didn't make fun of me or even suggest I was an idiot. He just tried to set me up with other girls who were more compatible. Remembering the good times we had together makes me appreciate the terrific friendship we shared. But for many years I focused mainly on the bad memory of letting him down, and felt like a terrible person. Again, through therapy I learned to focus more on remembering the positive memories I have of knowing Phil, and not so much on the negative ones.

Both Renee and Phil saw value in me and, whether I realized that or not, and they had an extremely positive effect on my life. I was magnetically drawn to their positive energy when I was growing up because at home and school I was surrounded with mainly negative energy. I wanted to feel better about myself when I was a kid, and when I spent time with them I felt great. Yes, I have some bad memories of my relationships with them, but not from anything they ever did. I tortured myself remembering what I perceived I had done or said. The impact of having known them and of having developed great relationships with them lasted long after they moved away and we lost contact. As an ADDer, I now know that we seek positive reinforcement and we do not judge where that positive reinforcement comes from. We take it and grab onto it and I will do just about anything for the person who provides that positive reinforcement. On the other hand, when we receive negative reinforcement, regardless of the reasons for it, we get as far away from it as we can.

I recently remembered a wonderful memory of Phil where he demonstrated his loyalty to me. Phil loved taking risks and excitement, and from time to time got in trouble for it. I would always go along with him because he did things that stimulated my mind. I never told him not to do something or said what he was doing was crazy. He liked that, and I think that's a reason he chose to be around me rather than others who would have judged what he was doing. One time I participated in one of his schemes and he took the complete blame for it. We had some firecrackers, and as we walked by someone's house, I put one of the larger firecrackers into a mailbox. Phil and I ran around the corner to listen for the loud explosion. It was exhilarating for me, and it was the first and last time that I actually participated in one of Phil's pranks. Phil never encouraged me to participate in or do the things he did. I guess he wanted to protect me, in his own way. After we walked for a while away from the firecracker incident, a car came screeching to a halt in front of us. A guy got out of the car and started yelling at us. Apparently, it was the owner of the house, and the mailbox. Phil told him that he was the one who put the firecracker in his mailbox and then took off running like the wind. I knew he would not be caught. He could run like no other I had ever met. The guy got back in his car and pursued him. Phil cut through gardens and backyards, and the guy never caught him. I continued walking casually to Phil's house, and was never bothered by the guy in the car. When I got to Phil's house, he was already there. He told me about his adventure running through the backyards and gardens. He laughed while he explained how he had to hide in a chicken coup for a few minutes. Then he told me never to do what he did. Phil appreciated our friendship and did not want me to get in any trouble. He knew what my father would do to me if I ever got into any kind of mischief. I only wish I had understood Phil back then the way I understand him today.

It is not only my childhood memories that affect me. I have a very recent memory of not understanding my boss by missing certain communication cues he was giving me. My boss pulled me aside one day to discuss a situation with me and informed me that I needed to act more mature. He did not tell me directly that I needed to grow up, but indirectly and at length. At the time I did not understand what he was saying to me because he told me using subtle metaphors and similes to describe what he meant. I just did not get the between-the-lines message he was trying to send me. My boss thought I was being stubborn and rebellious when it was obvious to him that I did not understand the situation he was describing and what he meant. I let him think I was being rebellious because I did not understand him, because as an ADDer, I was just trying to get by and did not want to ask for a clearer explanation. If I had understood him then, I would have certainly taken his advice and done things differently. That was a tough personal and professional recommendation to take in when I finally deciphered his meaning. When I looked back on the situation, which is only about two years ago, I cringed at the thought of it. With a better understanding of my ADD, I understand why it was so difficult for me to get the subtlety of his message.

I have learned to survive at work, for the most part by keeping some of the more challenging ADD traits that I have to myself, even before I was diagnosed with it. Since I have been diagnosed with ADD, I still keep my shortcomings to myself. Most of my coworkers perceive me as arrogant and standoffish because I do not engage in idle conversations with them. I did however, let my current boss know that I have ADD, and that has helped me more effectively communicate with him. He explains what he expects from me directly and in a more matter of fact manner. By him doing this I can accomplish assignments more efficiently without trying to second-guess exactly what he wants. He also gives me many assignments that highlight the highly creative aspect of my ADD. I have achieved a lot of success in my job, but I know that I should be at a higher level than I currently am. I feel like I have held myself back because I have misunderstood many subtle cues and explanations over the years from other bosses. I was never great at office politics either.

It is exasperating to think back about all of the times I have made repeated mistakes in my life due to a miscommunication with someone. I used to berate myself for making such unnecessary mistakes because sometimes these mistakes were detrimental to me getting a promotion, making a new friend, keeping a friend, or worse. As a child, my mistakes cost me free time by being put on restriction or caused me to be physically punished by my father. It can be very difficult to deal with, even at an age where I have come to understand I have a learning disorder. It is no wonder that grownups diagnosed with ADD/HD are also diagnosed with depression or PTSD. Finally being diagnosed and learning about ADD has been a watershed event in my life. Once I began to learn about my ADD, I discovered ways to cope with its symptoms even better than before, by learning what kind of changes I can make to get along better at work and in my personal life.

14

Improving Relationships

I have hurt some people in my life and personal relationships were challenging for me when I was not aware that I had ADD. Since I have been diagnosed with ADD, I consider how the symptoms of my disorder may affect others, and in doing so, I am able to have more fulfilling personal relationships with the people I care about most. My ADD traits still exist, however with therapy and a keener knowledge of my limitations and abilities, I have learned how to relate to others with more consideration of my ADD. I am able to communicate far more effectively with others because I make an effort to listen closely to what they are saying and take the time to absorb it first, before I respond. This is no easy task for someone who is easily distracted and is used to tuning out others. I also try to be more organized every day. I know I have not changed completely over night, but the changes I have made have been well worth it. My relationships are not in constant conflict due to simple misunderstandings and miscommunication. Making a positive effort to nurture my relationships, instead of dismissing them out of frustration and lack of understanding, enriches my life in a way I never thought possible.

My parents were frustrated with my behavior as a child and, as a result, disciplined me and continually told me I was lazy. When I got older, I tried to punish my father for the way he treated me by alienating him from my life. Although I continued to talk to my mother, I knew she was still disappointed with me as a young adult. Her constant criticism of the way I chose to live my life created dissonance between us that made it difficult for us to have a closer relationship for many years. I love my mother and loved my father, and I wanted to have a good relationship with them when I was younger. I tried to reconcile with my father before he died the best way I knew how before I knew I had ADD. My mother still tries to give me advice, which I now consider as her way of showing me how much she cares. My mother and I are closer now than we ever were because we are beginning to understand each other better. I appreciate that she just wants the best for me.

Carmen, my ex-wife, also wanted the best for our marriage. She wanted me to be someone I was not; she constantly reminded me that I didn't do things the way they should be done. When we first got married, I tried to change some of my quirks to make her happy. However, I could not meet her high expectations. She did not understand why I was so disorganized and inattentive. She was conflicted and angry when I would not adhere to a structured home life, follow her prescribed rules of life, or follow through on my responsibilities. I cared about her, but I ended up finding ways to avoid her pedantic criticism. I know I hurt Carmen by not being the kind of husband she wanted me to be. I ended our relationship not yet understanding who I was or why I did things in a certain way. It was not only painful for me not to be accepted for who I am, but also for not understanding why. For a while I thought it would be best if I lived alone, not needing to please or be responsible for anyone.

Then I met Joan, my wife, my love, my complement. Some people are meant to be together and some people are not, regardless of any disorder or peculiar behavior one might have. Joan and I are simply good together and that has a lot to do with how supportive she is as a person. Understanding is critical to our relationship and even with it, some circumstances can still be painful. Love, therefore, is the foundation of our marriage. I have never felt so intuitively connected or cared so much for someone before I met her. I can talk to her about anything at anytime. Indeed, meeting Joan changed my life.

Joan is supportive of me in every way, and she loves to boost my self-esteem. She is the one person in my life who has inspired me to be a better man. Her goal is not to change me, but to enhance our relationship by bringing out the best in me. Her passionate nature beckons my mind and heart simultaneously. She has introduced me to a completely new world of philosophy, history, art, and science. She has also helped me learn how to care about people, and has shown me that it can be safe to care. Not everyone is out to punish, condemn, and criticize.

I do not respond well to negative criticism or chastisements; I tend to become defensive or dismissive when I get them. When I make a mistake or am upset about something, Joan doesn't lecture me or criticize me. She patiently listens to me and asks me questions about the situation or my feelings. Many times I respond by saying that I am not sure why I do certain things or respond to situations the way I do because that's the way I have always done things. If I ask her, she suggests ways I can accomplish things more efficiently or deal with situations more thoughtfully. She doesn't force me to change my behavior, she asks me to think about the positive results of changing certain behaviors. She has helped me understand that a person can change certain things about themselves if they become aware of it and have the desire to change.

Prior to me being diagnosed with ADD, Joan's observations of me on a daily basis led her to suspect that I might have an underlying issue. She recognized that I became frustrated and angry with myself when I did not understand something or when I could not find the motivation to accomplish something. At her suggestion, I scheduled an appointment with a doctor specializing in treating learning disorders. Joan hadn't offered to name what disorder could be causing me to have such difficulties and she really didn't know, but she did convince me that it would be a good idea to check into and rule out certain conditions. She knew I had already undergone therapy to help me with my childhood traumas, but she pointed out that blaming my childhood for all of my behaviors might not be the wisest thing and that I should seek a another opinion considering my habits and traits. Something I had not considered was also something she pointed out to me: the difficulties I had in my childhood primarily began when I started to go to school, where my poor performance was then punished for years until I finally moved out. Joan and I talked about everything, including things I was very uneasy discussing with others before. Even so, it just seemed right to talk to her about these things. She was patient, helpful, and showed sincere concern for my well-being. She had already raised an intelligent, emotionally well-adjusted son, and I think that is why she so understood when I opened up to her about my most painful, personal issues.

Joan is well educated and an artist. I have always had a highly creative streak in me, but never gave it much consideration. Joan recognized my creativity as a gift and admired it in the things I did when I didn't even realize I was being creative. I have always been into colors, especially pastels, and use them in various ways to help me remember things. I did this even before I knew what ADD was. In the past, I created advertisements for my company. Joan saw some of them on my computer and thought that they were brilliant. She claimed that I was extremely creative. I disagreed because I could never draw or paint in the manner with which she did. Her art is, in my opinion, gallery worthy and I just put stuff together. She explained that what I put together, especially with the colors I used, was very exciting and captivating. I simply put things together that I would be attracted to; I really did not put too much effort into my designs because I would usually become bored with it rather quickly. In order to stay interested in my assigned projects, I would usually create advertisements using color combinations that would grab my attention.

I love my wife; she is unique in so many wonderful ways. She is there for me and for the first time in my life I am there for someone else – her. I guess I have always needed someone who is patient, supportive, and especially non-critical. We are in constant contact with each other, and thanks to modern technology, it is very easy to be. We're always calling, text messaging, and emailing each other. In fact, if we had met at any time before cell phones and email, we do not think our relationship would have worked out. We met doing our jobs and texting back and forth. She lived in another city nearly an hour away. Although we lived in different cities and it was not easy to meet, we remained in constant contact. What was fascinating to me was that she was able and is still able to keep my attention. She's not perfect and she does not pretend to be. Often our imperfections are what hold our attention and require our combined efforts to help us improve each other. I felt such a strong desire to be with her that I drove to her city nearly every day before we moved in together, and she drove to meet me with equal frequency. We were like two stars colliding and there was nothing that could keep us apart. I had never had that before in my life. I never felt such an intense attraction to someone that I absolutely had to be near as often as possible.

Being with Joan is a testament to the law of attraction, and how well this universal law works. I have always wanted to be with the type of woman that Joan is. She is caring, loving, and most importantly, she is understanding. Joan has come into my life and helped me in ways that no other has. She is smart, unpredictable, and exciting. When we talk about the way we met, we both believe it was meant to be. At the time, we were looking for someone and the universe moved to bring us together. Before we met, we lived two completely separate lives and grew up in two very different ways. We met simply by chance on the phone one evening when she was calling my office on behalf of a customer. Nothing happened between us right away, but two weeks later when she called to follow up for the customer, I fortunately got to help her again. She sent me an email thanking me for my efforts, and I wrote her back. Not too long after that, I ended up in her city for some reason and asked her to join me for a cup of coffee. From the moment we first made contact through the initial phone call, it did not seem there was any way for us not to remain in contact. At one point after we started seeing each other as much as possible, she decided that the constant commute was so physically wearing on her that we would have to stop seeing each other. After she decided this and drove back to her city, a muffler happened to come off another car and she drove over it. Her car became damaged and she had to stop on the side of the road. Because she was still close to my house, she called me and I came out to help her. We decided at that moment that she should move in with me and seek a job in my area. We have been together ever since.

Since meeting Joan, I feel that for the first time in my life I am coming to understand myself and, at the same time, I am caring for someone else. It's a great feeling and I am deeply grateful we found each other.

15

Rediscovery

It's a very emotional experience taking pen to paper, writing about my life. At the same time, it's been very gratifying to see where I was and how far I've come. It is not possible to change the past, even if I wish at times that I could. However, it is possible to learn from the past and this book is my attempt to do that, and at the same time offer my personal insights to you and others. Writing this book is also a huge risk for someone who is inherently sensitive to criticism. Taking risks is part of the ADD mind and this risk of emotional and personal exposure is a risk worth taking.

A diagnosis is the most important part of treating and dealing with ADD. There is a variety of symptoms that ADD shares with other disorders. If a person has had ADD for most of his life and it's gone undiagnosed, he or she could also be suffering from other issues, such as depression. A major reason that I was not diagnosed earlier in life is that everyone has some ADD/HD traits. Determining a diagnosis for ADD/HD is complex. Just because a person has a trait or two of ADD/HD does not mean the person has ADD/HD. My doctor took years of my medical, educational, and family history to help form the ADD/HD conclusion. I am essentially a very healthy person physically. I went through multiple medical tests to rule out other conditions, which cause similar symptoms. My thyroid function was tested, I had a full MRI scan, had multiple series of blood tests done, and went through many other comprehensive physical and mental exams for months before my doctor reached his diagnosis of ADD. I also answered lengthy questionnaires about my personality traits and character. At first, my doctor was concerned that I might be a hypochondriac. According to one of my doctors, many adult ADD/HD sufferers come across as hypochondriacs. People who have ADD/HD know they are having problems, and when they seek medical advice, doctors not understanding ADD/HD who give them clean bills of health, tell them that their illness is just all in their heads. Well yes, actually it *is* in our heads! Being told that there was nothing wrong with me physically was a relief, but I had a strong belief that there was some underlying issue to the way I was. After extensive testing, I was finally diagnosed with a manageable condition that was indeed in my head, Attention Deficit Disorder. It is no surprise that I did not give up trying to find an answer for my behaviors. ADDers can be persistent when they choose to focus on something.

My family history was examined with a fine tooth comb by my doctor. Thankfully I had years of therapy with Dr. Gary so I wasn't too shy about telling another doctor about my upbringing. Before therapy, I never mentioned my experiences growing up because I felt as though I was to blame for the way I was treated then. Moreover, I thought that talking about my painful and confusing childhood would upset my sisters and mother. I kept my feelings about the past to myself for a long time out of guilt and concern for my family. By doing this, my memories seemed to take on an uncontrollable life of their own in my mind. I ended up hurting myself more by blaming myself and staying quiet. `Keeping the peace´ was my motto for most of the years of my life.

Having my behavior suppressed by my father, and being quiet for so many years is another major reason I was not diagnosed earlier. My doctor revealed to me that most suspected ADD/HD sufferers are referred to a specialist dealing with ADD/HD when they are young because they are hyperactive in the physical sense, and therefore attract unappreciated attention to themselves. I am not hyperactive in the physical sense; I learned to survive by being a compliant child, keeping my mouth shut, and staying still. My punishments taught me to behave in that manner. I remember my parents constantly receiving compliments about how well behaved I was. I was quiet and still to avoid punishment. However, my mind remained ultra-hyperactive! Hence the reason I describe myself sometimes as ADD and sometimes as ADHD. Diagnosis required me to remember the reasons why I was punished, and exactly what it was that frustrated my father about me. By examining that, we learned that I probably had ADD/HD when I was very young, but my behavior was modified through my father´s extreme discipline. The symptoms I suffered from as a child and have now are mainly due to ADD.

For many people who suffer from the symptoms of ADD, diagnosis and treatment bring them some relief and understanding. When I was first diagnosed with ADD, I was skeptical. However, once I began to learn about ADD/HD, I began to agree with the diagnosis. As I gained more knowledge about the disorder from my doctor and my own research, a remarkable feeling came over me and I started to feel better about myself. I felt myself breathe a long, deep sigh of relief. Finally, I had an explanation for my ways! For so long I felt misunderstood and blamed myself for my innate traits, and I don't feel so alone in the world anymore. It was an enlightening experience for me. Finding out I have ADD gave me a clearer sense of direction, as though I had been wandering in circles for years and was finally handed a map to help guide me out of the confusing maze that was my life. At last!

When I let my therapist, Dr. Gary, know that I had been diagnosed with ADD, to my surprise he was not surprised and agreed with the diagnosis. He even acknowledged that sometimes it is good to seek a separate opinion. He appreciated my determination to find out more about behavior, and that my positive attitude contributed to my resourcefulness and ability to cope. Dr. Gary primarily treated me for depression and low self-esteem when I started seeing him, due to my childhood experiences. He concentrated on what he described as child abuse. It was his belief that my problems stemmed from my father's punishments and chastisements of me, and suggested that I

questions and get more involved in the conversation or activity. My goal is to relate better with others and to improve the relationships I have by not being so offensive in social situations.

With diagnosis of ADD/HD comes great responsibility to learn and adjust. Having ADD/HD does not mean I am inhibited from learning. As I mentioned, I do learn, just not in the same manner as most other people do. It has been of great importance for me to learn to get along with my ADD. I know I can be forgetful so I find ways to help me remember appointments, deadlines, meetings, and even social engagements. Using my computer and phone to set reminders for myself has been an easy way for me to remember those things. Modern technology is extremely beneficial to ADDers, and helped me stay more organized. ADD/HD sufferers who want to modify their behaviors are often advised to use what is available to them in the way of modern technology and to get assistance from a life coach to help them cope. My therapist also helps me by discussing some of the adjustments I want to make in my life. But day to day, my wife and mother help me the most with encouragement, advice, and reminders to keep me on track. I welcome the way my wife, Joan, helps keep me on track in my daily life. She coaches me and gives me advice in a positive way. She is an extremely intuitive person and knows how to talk to me and listen to my needs with compassion. My wife knows me better than anyone, and has already helped me in so many ways. I trust her advice, and love that she is always there for me with an ear to listen or a shoulder to cry on, when needed. My wife is my number one fan; she motivates me and gives me encouragement when I feel discouraged. Joan read my drafts of this book everyday, while I was writing it, and reminded me to add events that she knew were relevant to my story. She remembered everything I had told her about my struggles growing up and encouraged me to include what I had forgotten.

Joan has impressive organizational skills and when it comes to household paperwork, bills, and appointments, her assistance is a godsend. ADDers usually loath paperwork; organizing any sort of paperwork is one of our worst challenges. Our minds simply do not organize or catalogue information, especially mundane information, in an orderly or consistent manner. I have papers everywhere, and I do mean *everywhere.* My wife reminds me when bills are due and she prefers picking up the mail for us. I trust my wife and mother and am grateful to have electronic gadgets to help get me better organized, but I realize that there are going to be times that I will be forgetful despite my best efforts not to be. I still have to be aware that if I forget something, I will be the one held responsible. Society, companies, and especially bill collectors, will not accept a person having ADD as an excuse for missed appointments, cancelled meetings, or late payments. People who think in an orderly manner probably cannot imagine how the mind of a person who has ADD works. I believe that ADDers such as myself receive a lot of criticism for their forgetfulness and other innate behaviors because most people don't understand how ADD affects those who have it, or that the disorder is real.

Having an awareness of my ADD behaviors does not mean that I can modify all of them successfully on my own. I am impulsive at times due to my ADD, and controlling that aspect of my disorder has been a challenge. I still find myself saying what I think and acting on things too quickly without considering the consequences. To control impulsivity I don't really know if there is a way besides prescribed medication. Controlling my behavior is hard work and requires constant consideration and monitoring. I am learning some techniques though, which help delay my impulsive actions in certain situations. Before I talk, I try to remember to take a deep breath. Taking that breath gives me a second or two to consider what I am going to say before I blurt something out that I would rather not. With emails, I like to put them in draft after composing them for few minutes or longer before actually sending them. Before making expensive purchases, my wife and I talk about it and then sleep on the idea overnight. These are a few ways I try to deal with my impulsive behavior without medication.

Although I can focus well on things that interest me, I still get distracted and have trouble concentrating on regular tasks. To help me stay more consistently focused every day, I take small amounts of ginseng. It's not a perfect remedy for everyone, but it does help me concentrate better and feel less distracted. My doctor prescribed me an antidepressant, a selective serotonin reuptake inhibitor (SSRI), to help improve my mood and concentration. I took the SSRI for six weeks but the side effects of the drug were too much for me to handle. I stopped taking that SSRI medication cold turkey one day without tapering off the dosage and suffered extreme withdrawal effects for months. A word of warning to anyone using medication to treat a condition: if you want to stop taking it, discuss it with your doctor first. Only take medication prescribed by your doctor, and consult him or her before taking anything to treat an illness or disorder. Besides ginseng and a multi-vitamin, I don't take any other medication. I may decide to try other medication in the future, but for right now, I am learning ways to cope with some my ADD symptoms through behavioral and cognitive therapy sessions with my doctor.

I also try to pay more attention to the time. Daydreaming for me is something I just *do*. It is a benefit to my creativity and I can do it with such vivid clarity that it's almost like watching a movie. Daydreaming, for me, has always been a pleasant way to escape daily distractions. My doctor encourages me to talk about the past with him in order to release it so that I can live a more fulfilling life now. Staying in the present seems to give me more of a life. Because of the constant distractions, daydreaming and being impatient, it always seems like I miss days, weeks, months, and even years. I am so used to trying to tune out all of the activity around me that I rarely take in the moment and appreciate experiences as they are happening. For me, time just flows by and passes unnoticed. I am working and doing things, and then suddenly I look up and wonder where the time went. ADDers are typically not great time managers. What I do more often is actually look at the clock, think about what I am doing, where I am, who I am with, and take in the moment. When people start talking to me for any reason, I pay more attention to what they are saying and become engaged in the conversation. I have discovered that taking the time to appreciate individual moments in the present enriches my daily life, and helps me feel better about myself.

I have learned to forgive myself for mistakes I made. Beating myself up every day and regretting the past is not a good way to live. Having ADD is not an excuse, but it is a reason for exhibiting certain behaviors. Understanding there is a reason for my actions is the most influential way for me to cope. Forgiving others is also as important. I realize that it is very difficult to know how another person thinks about things or processes information. My actions and behaviors as an ADDer were often infuriating and confusing to others. Many times I would get bored with what people had to say, mentally dismiss them, and would not take the time to register their opinion in my mind. I don't want to be frustrating and rude, so I try to communicate more clearly now and consider others opinions. I have also learned to observe my tact. There is no reason to hurt another person's feelings. I have hurt people's feelings simply by not realizing that my thinking is different. I have learned to apologize. Apologies are not always accepted, but it does make me feel better knowing I made the effort and maybe when I try harder the people will realize I genuinely meant my apology. I am still learning ways to cope and it is a relief to know that there are many ways I can make positive changes in my previously inexplicable behaviors.

Support of one's family is critical for a person with ADD/HD. With the presence of undiagnosed ADD, a lot of misunderstandings and stress can hurt family relationships.

I've illustrated that here in my story. My sisters and mother are supportive of me, but my father was also supportive of me in his own way. I understand today that he thought he was disciplining a child who was disobedient. Maybe his method of discipline was excessive and it is not for me or anyone else to judge him. If I could write the story of my life without writing about my father's actions upon me, which did shape much of my life, I would.

My father had his own inner turmoil and I will never know how much his actions against me affected him. I think that if I had grown up in today's world I might have been treated differently. I am certain that my father cared for me in his own way. Therefore, I am moving forward with better understanding of myself, knowing that I love my father more now than I ever had. He raised three children and we never went hungry or without clothing on our backs. My father always provided for us well. Whenever any of us were sick or showed symptoms of being ill, my father would stop whatever he was doing and attend to us. Knowing how he was when we got sick makes me think that if I had been diagnosed with a medical disorder back then, he would have treated it seriously. Although he had a temper and his punishments were harsh, I feel he did the best he knew how to do. Today there is more emphasis on advising parents not punish children using violence or verbal abuse than there was when I was growing up. The movement to stop physically punishing children was a new and progressive concept when I was a kid in the 70's. Most people still believed back then that if you spared the rod, you'd risk spoiling the child. My father passed away a few years ago and I have learned to forgive him. Learning to reconcile my past has helped me move forward in my life in a more positive way.

I can't imagine how my mother managed to raise three successful children, especially with one as confusing as I was. I can't imagine what she must have gone through caring for me and maintaining a good relationship with my father. I know she did her best for me and did not realize that I had ADD as a child. What is important to me is the love and support my mother has given me over the years. When I was eighteen and moved out of the house, she still tried to take care of me by cooking for me, helping me financially, and by giving me good advice. My mother, who is a retired psychiatric nurse, is a very well educated woman. Even with her education and training as a nurse, she was not aware of ADD/HD when I was growing up. To her, I seemed like a perfectly healthy child who did not want to do as I was told by my parents. I grew up in a good home with a psychiatric nurse for a mother and my behavior was as confusing to her as it was at times frustrating. Through it all, she tried to understand me and protect me and she always loved me.

Growing up I did not have much contact with my sisters. My older sister is nearly three years older than I am, and my younger sister, is five years younger than I am. When we were kids, we lived in the same house and ate at the same dinner table, but we lived completely separate lives. That's not really a surprise considering our age differences. We didn't share the same friends or ever see each other at school. It wasn't until we grew up and were out of the house that we started to establish closer communication with each other. I am closer with them now as an adult. My sisters are supportive of me and they always have been. I know they would like me to stay in touch with them and their children more often. Nonetheless, in typical ADDer style, there are times when I am in contact with them continuously, and then there are times when I don't contact them for months. I want to communicate with them more consistently. Knowing I have ADD, I understand why I am the way I am and that I can work to improve my neglectful behavior. It motivates me to work my mind in a direction which is more considerate and appropriate, especially when it comes to my family.

Although parents have the most influence on a child's development, people outside the family can also have some affect on a child's intellectual and emotional growth. A child, even with an early diagnosis of ADD, may still be misunderstood by those outside of the family as lazy, irresponsible, or stupid. Parents, who learn that their child has ADD, will be more likely to understand his or her particular behaviors and help them overcome some of the difficulties of ADD to become productive and emotionally well-adjusted adults. They will be more likely to nurture their child, whereas others may chastise and punish an ADDer's academic performance or antics. Parents can try to shelter their child the best they can, but as the child grows up and begins to go to school and socially develop, they will be exposed to harsh criticism for the way they are from those who don't understand it or believe ADD is a real disorder. Eventually an ADD child will have to deal with the world on his or her own with or without a diagnosis of the disorder. However, early diagnosis of ADD is ideal, and can help a child thrive in an unforgiving world. An ADDer will always have challenges to overcome, but strong positive support from their parents when they are young can increase an ADDer's confidence and self-esteem, which will help them cope with the negative criticism, deal with misunderstandings, and handle their mistakes in a more emotionally healthy way. Children with an early diagnosis of ADD can also learn early to understand and focus their brilliant innate talents due to their disorder more positively and productively.

ADDers are creative and are drawn to highly stimulating activities and things, and they tend to create things that are interesting and captivating to themselves as well as others. After all, if we have an attention deficit, then we need things that grab our attention! If it takes a very high stimulus to attract our eyes, ears, and other senses, then just imagine how stimulating our creations are for others who aren't as difficult to engage. We are instinctively creative and what we produce is never typical or average. Most ADDers I have met and read about catch a lot of grief for the ways that they are and especially when it draws attention to themselves. We don't do what we do to cause problems or to bring any disfavor to ourselves. We naturally attract and are attracted to colorful, dazzling, and eye-catching things and people that are interesting to look at and think about. It's not something we do consciously or deliberately. Consider Paris Hilton. She is a world famous person with ADD who draws a lot of attention to herself and has been since she was young. Most ADDers like myself have been attracting attention to themselves all of their lives, but not purposely or to be obnoxious. Paris Hilton mentioned in an interview once that she does not know why the press and public give her so much attention for just being herself. I know it is very hard to believe that we don't do it purposely; it merely happens that way, much like walking and talking. To us, the things we do seem very simple that just about anyone could do it and doesn't seem to warrant the attention it brings. Most ADDers are usually criticized harshly for our failings and so, when we do something which attracts positive attention and praise, we tend to do more of it, even if we are hated for our success.

I am good at creating successful advertising and marketing campaigns, and people often ask me to teach them how to do the same. I can teach some of what I do to others, but not everything because what I am able to create comes naturally to me and it is not something I have learned formally. Because I cannot easily relate what I know, some people get frustrated with me and think I do not want to share my knowledge or the secrets to my success. The way an ADDer uses his mind to achieve success is a unique process that cannot necessarily be mimicked by someone without ADD. Just as the people who come to me for such advice cannot seem to achieve the results I achieve, so can I not fully achieve the results that they achieve with their talents. We all try to achieve success with the talents and mental abilities we were born with. I have had people get mad at me, even to the point that they hate me and accuse me of being an attention hog. I do not think it is fair for anyone, whether they have ADD or not, to be disliked or ridiculed for their innate abilities. It may be annoying to others when someone constantly stands out ahead of the rest for what they do effortlessly. Nevertheless, it is just who we are. Attracting attention for our creative abilities is probably the most prominent trait of an ADDer.

It was only by chance that I started to do advertising for my company when I happened to walk into the office of one of my superiors who was creating an advertisement. As I watched him create the advertisement, I noticed that he became frustrated with the time it involved. He mentioned to me that he did not have the time to create a great ad and that he didn't feel it was really his forte anyway. To be helpful, and because I had some experience creating ads for my father's business, I offered to create the ad for him. The ad I created for him turned out well, and was presented to the top manager of our division, who was impressed with my work. Shortly after that, our top manager asked me to create all of our print ads as well as our company radio ads. The advertising work I did was well received and lauded for their effectiveness in increasing customers and sales by my boss and at the highest levels of our company. Even organizations that worked with us started to ask for my creative assistance. When I started doing the advertising for my company, I began to enjoy my work more and appreciate the opportunities for advancement that were coming my way. I was encouraged to enroll in the upward mobility program, my company's junior management course, which I completed at the top of my class. I was soon promoted to a management position where my advertising ability was not needed as much. As a manager, I continued to create exciting and popular radio advertising for my departments. From the time I first started advertising for the company, years would pass during which I was promoted into other management positions where I focused on other job responsibilities before I would once again be asked to do advertising for the company. I was asked to be the Public Affairs Representative and to be responsible for their local marketing campaign by creating and sending out weekly mass email advertisements. In addition to my duties as a manager, I successfully accomplished advertising and marketing campaigns which were consistently praised at the highest corporate level for their creativity, professionalism, and effectiveness at increasing customer awareness and sales. Moreover, I recently received the company's highest award for my outstanding performance in both areas.

I perform better overall when I have something interesting on which I can focus my creative energy. I have found that the ability to hyper focus is a useful trait, which allows me to become deeply involved in something I enjoy. When my mind is in hyper focus mode, I can become an expert in almost any given subject. It doesn't seem to matter what the subject is, it just matters that I am interested in it. With the diagnosis of ADD, I have even learned there are ways I can turn on and turn off my hyper focus ability. I have learned to control it by using it when there is something particularly interesting that I want to learn or create. Deep breathing exercises help me get into my hyper focus mode. When I found out that deep breathing exercises are commonly recommended to help a person with ADD concentrate, I almost wanted to slap myself on the forehead and say "duh!" I used that technique before I was diagnosed with ADD to help me with focus on my pool game. Years ago, when I won my first major pool tournament, I happened to be taking a Tai Chi class. Tai Chi is a martial arts form with an emphasis on calm motion, controlled breathing, and meditation. Learning Tai Chi was a great experience for me; it taught me how to calm my body and mind, which enabled me to use my ability to hyper focus in a more productive way. Ironically, I originally stopped taking Tai Chi classes because I thought they were boring. I did not realize the benefits I got and used from the exercises I was taught. Today, when I need to concentrate or clear my mind, I take a moment to relax and breathe deeply the way I learned in my Tai Chi classes.

When I use my creativity and hyper focus abilities at the same time, I can produce some incredible things. I remember when I was younger, especially at times when I was restricted or grounded to my room, I would draw, write short stories, rearrange my room in fun new ways, and make animals out of string. My mother loves to knit and we have always had lots of yarn around the house. When I had nothing else to use I would ask my mom for some yarn and she would give me as much as I wanted. I would take a long string of yarn and begin to make knots in it. Eventually these knots would begin to form a figure. I would create dogs, cats and many different forms with the yarn, but none of them was preplanned. I usually had no specific direction I wanted to go with my creations, they just turned out to be whatever I decided they looked like. My dad really liked my creations, and would often ask me to create something specific around the house, like a chair or a lamp, but I had a lot of difficulty creating anything specifically requested. Later, when I worked for my father's business, he had me do some advertising for him. I remember him being pleased with my ads, and yet he always had some kind of criticism of how I could do them better or tone them down. Often people would come to my dad's business and ask who created the ads. My dad loved to brag about my great signs, but I only created them for him and wouldn't do it for anyone else. Had I been diagnosed earlier with ADD and had more confidence in my innate creative abilities and myself back then, I probably would have gone into advertising. From what I have read and been told, many ad and marketing agencies seek out people with ADD/HD specifically for the way their creative minds work.

Superior multi-tasking is another great attribute of ADD. My mind is always going full steam ahead and needs constant stimulus to keep it from getting bored. At work, having a demanding primary job as a manager, plus accomplishing additional advertising and marketing duties helped me tremendously to do better work overall. However, performing well does not prevent me from having difficulties at work. A few years ago, a top manager met with me and explained that although he believed I must have a very high IQ, he believed I lacked maturity. I can't tell you how dramatically this statement filled me with pride and shame at the same time. His analysis of me was humiliating and confusing. At the time I didn't understand how I seemed immature to him or how I could be more mature. I was upset with that manager for a while until I was diagnosed with ADD. When I reconsidered what he said, I felt enlightened by his comment and now appreciate that he took the time to talk to me. This just continues to show how important the diagnosis of ADD has been for me, for now I consider certain criticism with respect to my disorder and how others may perceive my behavior. From what I understand, many ADDers have very high IQs and yet as adults seem immature for their age. It is impossible to change one's personality completely, and therefore it is a good idea to let others know that you have ADD. When I let my managers at work know that I have this disorder, and that I am doing my best to improve my behavior every day and to excel professionally, they responded to the news supportively. Having ADD is not an excuse for bad behavior and it does not entitle anyone to special treatment; it is a reality and way of life for those who have ADD.

16

A New Day, A New Life

One of my favorite imagined fantasies as a child was to be a superhero with amazing, unlimited powers. In my mind, I could travel the universe righting wrongs and helping others. If I had a choice of the one thing I would not give up as an ADDer, it would be my imagination. It is nothing short of amazing. I truly appreciate my creative mind. I think of my creativity as one of my superpowers. My imagination has always been the place I could go to for solace, peace, and happiness.

It has helped me immensely to consider more of my positive traits since I have been diagnosed with ADD. My positive traits benefit me, and I like knowing that I can assist others and myself with my abilities. I call them my superpowers, a perceptional term I use to lift my self-esteem. Now I try to think more positively about my future and myself than I did in the past. Positive thinking did not come to me naturally; for years I had a negative outlook on life and myself because of my childhood experiences and the way I felt about myself. As an adult, I was fortunate to meet some great people who sincerely cared about my well-being. It was not until I read Norman Vincent Peale's book, *The Power of Positive Thinking,* that I realized I needed help. Reading that book inspired me to seek therapy, which was one of the most important decisions I ever made toward making significant positive changes in my life.

Before I began seeing a therapist I didn't exactly know why I was such a pessimistic person and I didn't try to figure it out on my own. However, I knew I wanted to be a more positive person, so I did read several books on the subject of positive thinking. Most of the books were informative, but seemed like a textbook of instructions. I didn't follow the lessons consistently or feel like I was learning anything from the generalized lists of ways to think more positively. I learn more from reading about someone's experiences. I easily related to and learned from many of the peoples' experiences that Peale describes simply and eloquently in *The Power of Positive Thinking.*

Nevertheless, I knew I needed more help than I could get from a book. I was even cynical when I first started seeking professional help. I met with two therapists with whom I did not feel comfortable before I met Dr. Gary, the type of therapist I was looking for. He was easy to talk to on a personal level, non-judgmental, and believed in positive reinforcement. Still, I had no idea what therapy would do for me or how important it really was. I would soon find out though, and for the first time in my life, I faced my inner angst. Dr. Gary asked me questions that I never thought to ask myself, or was too fearful to face on my own. He encouraged me to discuss difficult issues which were holding me back from living a positive, more fulfilling life. He not only asked me what I thought about my life and myself, but he also had me examine the reality of those thoughts and beliefs. I did not realize I had such negative beliefs, and I know I would have never fully overcome them without Dr. Gary's help. He helped me understand that I was not at fault for things which happened to me as a child, and that I could stop blaming myself for not being a good child. I had not considered the affects of my childhood on my adult emotions and mannerisms before I talked to him. I did not realize before that I had been holding on to resentments and shame from my past. Therapy helped me let go of some of my past issues and learn to think differently about them. It helped me identify some of my incessant negative thoughts and beliefs, examine them, and reconsider them from a new, more positive perspective. Dr. Gary helped me resolve many issues by having me talk about them aloud with him.

Having the therapy was like waking up to a brand new, sun-shiny day and being able to see clearly all of life's opportunities ahead of me. I started to feel better about my future and myself, but I was stuck in a pattern of behavior that I had trouble improving, no matter how positive I tried to be. Dr. Gary believed I still had troubling beliefs and thoughts hidden deep within my subconscious, and recommended that I continue with the therapy sessions. At the time, he was treating me for depression and PTSD. Dr. Gary also believed that I was so used to my habits that it might take a long time to change them. What we didn't realize is that my so-called habits were actually traits I had due to a neurobiological disorder which I have had since childhood. Most of my problems with distraction, day dreaming, and other typical ADD symptoms had been with me for as long as I can remember.

When I was diagnosed with ADD by another doctor, I finally had an answer for my persistent behaviors. I felt as though a locked gate in my mind suddenly opened and released old fears, feelings of low self-esteem and negativity. The diagnosis of ADD explained why I continued to hyper focus on negative, self-defeating aspects of my life. It also explained, to my relief, why I repeatedly did things which I didn't want to do.

I tried to modify certain behaviors or thought patterns, without understanding why they were happening, by thinking more positively. I realized that my attempt to change was unrealistic when I found out that there was an underlying neurobiological disorder present. Thinking positively isn't a cure for ADD, but I believe it is critical to managing the symptoms of the disorder. I wanted to think positively and I wanted to have help, and those desires reverberated through my being and attracted to me the people who could help me. I believe in the Law of Attraction and that like attracts like. We draw to us that which we think of the most. That is what I believe. I always wanted to create beautiful, exciting, and attention-getting things. I still managed to gravitate toward doing great advertising on the side at work, even though it is not my primary job. I have wanted to do something creative since I was a small child, and it manifested into something I do, and do very well. I want to help others with ADD or help direct people to seek assistance from someone who can identify whether they have a condition or not. It is through my desire to help others that this book is written, and I find the ability to continue writing when so many other things are constantly distracting me.

I have been contemplating writing this book for months. As usual with me, I put the idea off. I tried a few times to begin writing, but by the third or fourth sentence I usually would become distracted, stop, and discontinue. Then one day while at lunch, some co-workers were discussing the Oprah show and about a book that she was promoting called *The Secret.* The title was interesting, so I asked them to elaborate. The book is about the Law of Attraction and how this universal law is the secret to living a fulfilling life. Oprah has probably helped more people through her television show than just about any other person, and for her to promote the book meant that at the very least, it contained meaningful and useful information. I was interested in reading more about the Law of Attraction, so as soon as the book came out I purchased a copy of *The Secret,* written by Rhonda Byrne. Reading this book gave me a better idea about what it is to think and feel in a positive way. The accounts of others real life experiences of how the Law of Attraction affected their lives was inspiring to me, and helped me gain a clearer understanding of how it has already affected my life, and how it can affect me now. When we think positively or feel good and allow positive emotions to course through our bodies, regardless of our situations, we attract positive things and people to us. The book shows several examples of how people, who positively visualized their goals and desires, were able to attain them more easily than if they thought negatively about them. I visualized writing this book about my life, completing it, and having it help people all over the world. That you are reading this book right now is a testament of how the Law of Attraction and positive thinking has enhanced my life. Positive thinking helps me refocus my energy on my goals in a more productive way, and has helped me manage some of my ADD traits to my benefit.

With what I have learned through therapy about the Law of Attraction and from the benefits of positive thinking, I have stopped relying on my anxiety and negative pressure as ways to focus on achieving my goals. As a child, worrying helped me stay focused on staying out of trouble. It seemed that whenever I relaxed and stopped worrying or forgot to worry and lapsed into distraction, I would invariably get in trouble for something. Later, as an adult I used my worry method to keep me sharp at work and at the pool table in order to succeed. The more risk I felt of failure, the more pressure I would put on myself to focus on the tasks at hand. Although my method worked for me, I have since learned through therapy that it is not an emotionally or physically healthy way to achieve success. I understand now why I would get frequent headaches, stomach cramps, and become completely emotionally exhausted trying to achieve my goals. Thinking more positively and understanding the Law of Attraction helps direct and enable me to focus more effectively in a less stressful way by first visualizing my desired goal and how I can accomplish it in my mind, and then working positively toward achieving it. By visualizing what I want to achieve first, my mind processes situations more thoughtfully and comprehensively. My ADD mind frequently wanders and I get distracted thinking about a multitude of different things that interest me. When I feel myself becoming distracted, I use deep breathing exercises that I learned from Tai Chi to bring my mind back to visualizing my goals. Visualizing what I want keeps my mind focused on the positive outcome of something in which I am keenly interested; achieving a desired goal. I have worried and put undue pressure on myself to be successful for so long that it had become a habit which I needed to break. Using a new, more positive approach to achieving success is one way I am able to slowly break that destructive habit. This new way of focusing is refreshing and gives me a unique sense of calm which I have rarely known.

Knowing I have ADD makes me more aware that the ways I do things were not always acceptable or considered as normal by others. By observing people and seeing how they accomplish things, I have always had an idea that I did things differently than the accepted norm. Sometimes I watch others working on things and I wonder how they accomplish what they do. For example, when I look at a beautiful building and try to contemplate how it was built, I cannot imagine what was required to build it or how it was completed. I appreciate the architectural design of a building and can easily imagine variations of the building structure and style. I can create architectural designs for buildings for a particular location or function, but understanding the process of constructing a building from start to finish is beyond the grasp of my mind. I find it fascinating to watch the process of a something being put together or built because it is not something that I can do well. I enjoy observing a building under construction and watching the workers prepare a foundation, lay bricks, and raise the roof, but ultimately I prefer to think about the overall design of the building that is being built. When I was younger, most of my friends liked to make model airplanes and cars from kits filled with fused together plastic pieces. I never got excited about putting together bits of abstract pieces of plastic to form a historical fighter jet or a champion race car replica. I preferred to daydream, write stories, or draw the ideas I had about incredible planes and rocket ships that the superheroes of my imagination might use for their adventures, or about fast sports cars I wanted eventually to drive as an adult. Some people criticize my preference to contemplate ideas and designs as laziness, but it is simply an inability to understand how some things are put together. Having a highly creative mind is a major part of my nature as an ADDer; it is part of everything I do, which may not be considered normal by others but I feel fortunate to have my creative abilities.

People with ADD/HD are thinkers and have many great ideas. When I work on advertising projects, I can create the designs and complete the layouts for publication with ease. Sometimes though, I have trouble making other ideas a reality. I can come up with the grandest design or a wonderful idea, but I usually need someone else to help me see them to fruition. Recognizing my limitations isn't as frustrating for me as it once was because I realized that I have extraordinary talents in other areas. I know I have great ideas, but I am not always able successfully to develop them into something tangible on my own. I don't consider it negatively when someone else can develop my ideas to create something which reflects my original vision. Writing this book is an idea I had after I was diagnosed with ADD and began to learn more about the disorder. I was inspired to help others who may have grown up undiagnosed with the disorder, and parents of children who may exhibit symptoms of the disorder. I know the heartache I experienced having undiagnosed ADD as a child, and writing about it is as much a way of helping others understand ADD/HD better for themselves as it is an emotional catharsis for me. While I am writing this book, knowing exactly what I want to express, I am not diligently paying attention to the proper use of punctuation and grammar. I have hired an editor to help me correct the technical errors I have made, thus helping me fully realize my original idea. In the past I was reluctant to ask for help with anything. Knowing I have ADD, I understand that I simply do not have the mind for doing certain things, and that I also have the mind for accomplishing incredible things.

Afterword

Today is very important to me. I have lived a life of having one foot in yesterday and one foot in tomorrow. I want to have both feet in today to live a more fulfilling life, and that is my promise to myself every morning when I wake up.

It is a struggle to slow myself down or change my type of thinking, and yet at least I now know what I am doing and why I am doing it. Finally, with a diagnosis and learning about my disorder, I feel I am up to the challenges. Sometimes it just helps to look myself in the mirror and tell myself I am having an ADD day and laugh at it. It seems to me that releasing energy is the best form of clearing my mind and bringing me back to my center. I use deep breathing exercises, walking, window-shopping, and even driving to help myself relax and give my mind a much-needed rest. When my mind is rested and ready for new information, I try to fill it with positive information. Having ADD, I have a natural tendency to focus and dwell on negative information; knowing this helps me concentrate on the positive aspects of my life.

Having been diagnosed with ADD, I have a clearer understanding of the way my mind works. I finally have an explanation for my actions, which I never really understood before. I am working with my therapist and studying the affects of this disorder to improve myself. Because of the way I grew up, I have the desire to help others understand ADD/HD. I have a wonderful wife whose companionship and compassion make each day a pleasure. I am very fortunate to work for a company that embraces the skills at which I excel. I have good friends and a supportive family.

When things get rough and I start to drift and dwell on the negative, I literally take a time out and think about the positives. I try to find something good in everything I do and all that which surrounds me each day. When I take this approach to life, each day I discover that I find more things to feel positive about rather than negative, and that is how I prefer my mind to work. I find that the more I think positively, the more things which are positive are drawn to me, evidence that the Law of Attraction is a force working in my life. Thinking more positively is a choice I am able to make today by understanding why I was so pessimistic before. With the encouragement of my therapist, I was able to talk about and reevaluate my self-defeating negative thinking.

There were so many times through the course of writing this book that I wanted to stop and give up, and there are many experiences I write about that causes me emotional distress. While writing parts of this book, I actually found myself reliving certain events in my mind and experiencing the painful feelings I had then all over again. Some days, writing about my past was emotionally overwhelming and I wanted to quit. I would also start thinking of all the bad things that could happen to me by writing about my personal experiences, and forget why I wanted to write the book in the first place. Mostly, I felt guilty about the things that happened to me and ashamed of who I was. Guilt is the fore bringer of negativity and self-defeat. There are many things for me to feel bad about, but living with feelings of guilt and shame for most of my life has literally kept me from accomplishing or even trying to accomplish many things. The blame I placed on myself for being the way I was is depressing and exhausting. Many of my negative thoughts made me feel like Sisyphus, who was condemned to roll a huge boulder up a hill, never successfully reaching the top before the boulder would roll back down the hill, forcing him to start the exhausting task all over again. For the longest time I blamed myself for being a bad child and making my father mad at me, thus believing that I deserved to be punished consequently for my behavior and poor academic performance.

Most of my life I have been extremely sensitive to criticism and felt embarrassed about almost everything I did. I did poorly in school and my father always seemed mad at me. I was ridiculed by friends, neighbors, schoolmates, and even people I didn't know. It was frustrating to have people who believed they knew what was going on in my mind and felt obliged to give me suggestions on how I could improve myself, why I should perform better at school, and that if I didn't change my ways, I would be a failure all of my life. Comments like these were so frequent that I usually just agreed with them to please them. I wanted everyone to be happy and pleased with me to the point that I even made fun of myself. I openly ridiculed myself to beat people to the punch. I didn't know what else to do and it sure didn't seem I could change. People got so used to my self-deprecating way that when I started therapy and began to exhibit a healthier self-esteem, people still wanted me to feel insecure. I stopped hanging out with the people who called themselves my friends who were not supportive of the positive changes I was making. I started to realize who my friends really were, and those who were just making themselves feel better by having a friend like me with low self-esteem. There came a point when I would not accept ridicule from anyone, and I would not allow jokes to be made at my expense. I might have gone along with the personal criticisms and mockery to make everyone happy before, but those days were over.

Standing up for myself and refusing to be ridiculed was a bold, positive step for me to take at the time. Ultimately, I'm glad I took it but I have to admit that at first my increasing confidence had serious ramifications for those around me and myself. I used to rely on others for their support because I felt that I could not stand on my own two feet. It didn't matter to me if those same people humiliated me because I believed I needed them and wasn't secure enough in myself to be without them. Sadly, they knew it. Many people credited the change in me to my first wife, Carmen. If that were the case, well then, I probably would still be with her. As it so happens, I started going to therapy while I was married to Carmen and, through therapy, I began to gain more self-confidence which was the beginning of the end of our marriage. She worried about the positive changes I was making and told me that I would leave her if I became more confident and self-reliant. She had a difficult time with my improved sense of self, and our relationship did not survive my transformation. Carmen was comfortable being in charge of both of us in the marriage, and she was used to telling me what to do and how to do it. She repeatedly corrected me by saying the same phrase, "That's not the way you are supposed to do it". I can't tell you how often I heard that, but it was a lot more than I care to count. I grew to resent that phrase. It had been that way from the start of our relationship, before I started therapy, and I let her be in charge and reinforced her parental tendencies over me for years. As I became more confident and aware of who I was, I began to notice that we had a lot more differences than I had ever realized before.

The improved confidence was a problem for me at home, but not at work. I began to be more assertive at work and do a better job. I used to go to work, do my job, and go home with little or no recognition that I had even been there. I used to like it that way. For a while the most recognition I would receive was for being late, being too slow, or from clowning around when I was bored. With my self-esteem increasing, I began to show up for work on time and, after awhile, I even went into work early. I used to be such a clock-watcher, waiting to go home. Then I noticed that I rarely watched the clock and instead ensured that my work was complete before I went home, even if I had to stay a little longer. In the workplace, the changes in my confidence were well received. My company recognizes those who want to achieve and strive to improve themselves professionally and personally. I never realized that the significant changes I was making were so necessary and that they would make such a difference in my life.

My wife, Joan, did not know me before I started my initial therapy with Dr. Gary. I met her after I made many personal and professional improvements, but before I knew I had ADD. She loves who I am and appreciates that I believe in myself. She´s also compassionate enough to realize the things that disturb me, such as many of the traits of ADD, which I never really understood until I received a diagnosis of ADD. She suggested that I seek a second opinion for the behaviors that were still troubling me. She is supportive and understanding, and believes in building me up with positive reinforcement. We do that for each other and this is the type of relationship in which I feel most comfortable. When two people support each other through the good and bad times, together they can achieve anything. We both have made mistakes, but we try to learn from them and move forward. Our marriage is one of honest communication, positive emotional support, and passion for one another. Being in a good relationship, I finally felt comfortable acknowledging to someone else other than my therapist that I didn't know why I did some of the things I did. Joan was confused sometimes too by my behavior. She noticed that I would repeatedly make the same mistakes, knowing that they were wrong from the first time I made them. Most people learn from their mistakes and try not to make them again. But it was when these repeated mistakes began to create enough conflict and damage in my life that I wanted to seek further professional help.

When my mind gets stuck on finding an answer to a question, I can end up searching until I find the answer. It can be frustrating for those with whom I interact on a daily basis. They know that I will not let go of something no matter how important or trivial it is. Although this diligence can be good in some instances, in others it's not. It is the subtle cues I miss, or sometimes it is the short email message which could have more than one meaning. I tend to see more into a situation than what might really be there and this causes me to react, question, or get frustrated and cause unnecessary conflict. It has helped to know that the ADD mind has a tendency to miss the subtle human communication cues which most people get. Those cues, written, spoken, or in body language, tend to go over my head. It is especially difficult with sarcasm, irony, and jokes which could be understood as serious. It is in these situations that I have the most difficulty and have caused unnecessary conflict. Sometimes I take a harmless joke as serious and start going over all the possible implications in my head. My hyper focus and analyzing abilities mentally seek out all possible meanings; if I feel that any of those meanings could possibly be against me, I become reactive and take action. This is not only because of ADD, but also because I grew up with a lot of painful criticism, and therefore could be easily offended. Now that I understand myself better and know why I do what I do, I try to evaluate such situations more thoughtfully, as if I was on fire and my life depended on it. In effect I stop, drop, and roll. I stop to think it out thoroughly, drop my emotions by calming myself and clearing my mind with breathing exercises, and then roll on to asking for an explanation, if necessary. That's my stop, drop, and roll. I have discovered that people generally do not mind being asked for clarification, but they do mind any conflict created without giving them the chance to clarify. The more I have done this and reduced conflict, the more I find myself being appreciated and treated with more respect and even fondness.

ADD is an explanation for the way my mind works, but using it or thinking of it as an excuse is not helpful. Taking responsibility for who I am is infinitely more beneficial for me than sulking and feeling sorry for myself. I have tried the sulking and feeling sorry for myself route, and it does nothing for me but reinforce my old feelings of worthlessness and despair. My goal is to move forward in my life, improve my relationships, and to think more positively about everything I do. Like attracts like, which applies to the negative as well as the positive. My life is so much better since I have made changes to my daily life as needed, and taken responsibility for the way I am with ADD. Modifying my behavior is not easy and I don't expect it to happen overnight, for I still make mistakes and become perplexed by certain situations. Yet each day seems brighter and I feel more productive and more positive overall.

We walk together, you and me. Thank you for reading.
Bryan Hutchinson
June 10, 2007

For more information about me, please, visit me at my Blog:
www.adderworld.com

Dear Phil,

You were the best friend I ever had growing up. I might not be here today had it not been for your friendship, support, and ability to cheer me up and boost my self-esteem. You were always helping and supporting people with your enthusiasm and good nature.

You were truly blessed, a person with a wonderful heart and splendid character. You truly are awe-inspiring! You will always be remembered.

Your best friend always,

Bryan

Phil passed away in 2006. It is in his memory that this book has been written.

Dream on Commander Mart

Dream on Commander Mart

Flow into a violet cloud of calm

Seal off from the universe constantly

Clicking on off on into mind, into senses

Firing crimson streams of chaos, burst...still

Breathe, hold lowered eyes, shut out flashpoint orange noise

Smooth the sine waves slithering neon between ears,

Tangling behind a pensive, cool yellow stare...still

Breathe, let them recede into lush azure vibrations,

Gently enliven imagination... still

Dream on Commander Mart

Fly to your felicitous emerald world

Sown with courageous deeds, heralded feats, true blush of love

Glistening silver prizes waltzing before your rapt attention

Assured rhythm, sensible steps, energizing time

Warmly engaging, embracing your eclectic thoughts.

Conquer the steely naysayers, express with no regrets

Profound declaration of awareness

Clearly awaiting your day, radiant

Golden leaves crown the astonishing victor.

Dream on Commander Mart

Joan Faith Hutchinson

October 14, 2007

Medical Disclaimer

I am not a doctor, psychiatrist, or psychologist. I am not trained to diagnose or treat ADD/HD or any other illness or disorder mentioned in this book. What I have written are my own theories and opinions based on my own experiences. If you feel that you can relate to any condition or symptoms mentioned, please seek the advice of a medical or trained professional with your concerns. Nothing I have written in this publication is intended to take the place of professional advice, diagnosis, and/or treatment of any disorder or illness. When I use the ADDer plurals and/or write 'we' and 'us' I use these terms loosely and ultimately only refer to my traits and my experiences. We are not all completely the same.

Bryan L. Hutchinson grew up with undiagnosed ADD. He is the creator and author of AdderWorld.com, a popular website dedicated to raising ADD ADHD awareness. He lives with his wife, Joan Faith Hutchinson.

For more information about Bryan, please visit: www.AdderWorld.com

CPSIA information can be obtained at www.ICGtesting.com
Printed in the USA
LVOW07s0434260913

354138LV00007B/170/P